Dart Essentials

Design and build full-featured web and CLI apps using
the powerful Dart language and its libraries and tools

Martin Sikora

PUBLISHING

BIRMINGHAM - MUMBAI

Dart Essentials

First published: May 2015

Production reference: 1190515

Published by Packt Publishing Ltd.
Livery Place
35 Livery Street
Birmingham B3 2PB, UK.

ISBN 978-1-78398-960-7

www.packtpub.com

Credits

Author
Martin Sikora

Reviewers
Lamoriniere Cedric
Rokesh Jankie
Hans Van den Keybus
Frederik Leonhardt
Marko Vuksanovic

Commissioning Editor
Taron Pereira

Acquisition Editor
Shaon Basu

Content Development Editor
Akashdeep Kundu

Technical Editor
Mrunal M. Chavan

Copy Editor
Stuti Srivastava

Project Coordinator
Milton Dsouza

Proofreaders
Stephen Copestake
Safis Editing

Indexer
Hemangini Bari

Graphics
Sheetal Aute

Production Coordinator
Shantanu N. Zagade

Cover Work
Shantanu N. Zagade

About the Author

Martin Sikora has been programming professionally since 2006 for companies such as Miton CZ and Symbio Digital in various languages, mostly PHP. Since 2012, he's been freelancing, working on projects in Python, PHP, Dart, Objective-C, and AngularJS. He's a Zend Certified Engineer and was a member of the winning team at Google Dart Hackathon 2012 in Prague.

About the Reviewers

Lamoriniere Cedric is a software engineer and a graduate from a French engineering school, who mostly uses C++ during his day job.

His taste for innovation has led him to try out a considerable amount of various web frameworks, technologies, and languages.

Among these languages, he has taken a strong interest in the Dart language for its ease of use and efficiency. It allows developers to get things done in a timely manner.

Rokesh Jankie graduated in 1998 with a master's degree in computer science from Leiden University, the Netherlands. He specialized in algorithms and NP-complete problems. Scheduling problems that can be NP-complete was his area of focus. He started working for the University of Leiden, ORTEC consultants, and Ponte Vecchio, and later, worked for Qualogy. At Qualogy, he used what he had experienced till that point to set up a product. Qualogy works in the field of Oracle and Java technologies. With the current set of technologies, interesting products can be delivered, and this is what QAFE is (refer to www.qafe.com for more information).

QAFE Inc. has a very dynamic team, which works in an agile way (going to production weekly, quickly adjusting to market needs, and so on). In the team, they don't distinguish between senior developers and junior developers, but they recruit very good software engineers. This gives a new dynamic to the team and makes it a great experience on a daily basis.

Books that Rokesh has worked on include *Dart in Action, Manning Publications,* and *HTML5 and CSS Responsive Web Design Cookbook* and *HTML5 Canvas Cookbook,* both by Packt Publishing.

I'm very grateful to my parents and my wife for supporting my enthusiasm for computer science. My 2-year old son inspires me to be the best dad, and he makes sure that I work hard to create a better future for him through the application of computer science topics in daily life and by sharing my knowledge on this subject. Reviewing this book is part of that journey.

Hans Van den Keybus is a Belgium-based Flash, Flex, and Google Dart developer, working for his one-man company called dotdotcommadot.

Although he started off creating simple games and animations for some well-known design companies, he got the most fun out of structuring the code behind it. His main areas of expertise are OOP, design patterns, and microarchitectures.

Currently, he's working on a major project developed in Google Dart for his customers MSC and Maersk.

Whenever he's not programming, Hans is probably playing some sketchy basement with his even sketchier grindcore band.

Frederik Leonhardt is a tech enthusiast and software engineer with more than 5 years of experience in Java, Java EE, and related frameworks. He likes to delve into new technologies, and he started using Dart with its first beta release in 2012.

He likes to contribute to the open source community and is currently working for Catalyst IT, a team of open source technologists. In the past, he has worked as a researcher for the Institute of Information Systems at the German Research Center for Artificial Intelligence, where he published papers on recommender systems and their application in the mobile health domain.

He recently moved to New Zealand and enjoys the relaxed Kiwi lifestyle and the beautiful outdoors, especially for tramping and photography.

Marko Vuksanovic is a consultant who specializes in software development and delivery. He received his master's degree in electrical engineering and computing from the University of Zagreb, Croatia, in 2009. He is currently employed by ThoughtWorks Australia, where he helps deliver outstanding products to clients. He has spent the last 10 years working with web applications, and during this period, he has been involved in numerous open source, as well as closed source, projects. He is very active within the Dart community and used to actively contribute to AngularDart projects. His other interests lie in the information security and machine-learning spaces.

When not providing services to clients, Marko spends time acquiring new skills, breaking things, reverse engineering, or enjoying some time off at one of Australia's beaches or a nearby tennis court.

www.PacktPub.com

Support files, eBooks, discount offers, and more

For support files and downloads related to your book, please visit www.PacktPub.com.

Did you know that Packt offers eBook versions of every book published, with PDF and ePub files available? You can upgrade to the eBook version at www.PacktPub.com and as a print book customer, you are entitled to a discount on the eBook copy. Get in touch with us at service@packtpub.com for more details.

At www.PacktPub.com, you can also read a collection of free technical articles, sign up for a range of free newsletters and receive exclusive discounts and offers on Packt books and eBooks.

https://www2.packtpub.com/books/subscription/packtlib

Do you need instant solutions to your IT questions? PacktLib is Packt's online digital book library. Here, you can search, access, and read Packt's entire library of books.

Why subscribe?

- Fully searchable across every book published by Packt
- Copy and paste, print, and bookmark content
- On demand and accessible via a web browser

Free access for Packt account holders

If you have an account with Packt at www.PacktPub.com, you can use this to access PacktLib today and view 9 entirely free books. Simply use your login credentials for immediate access.

Table of Contents

Preface

Since the first public release of Dart in 2011, the language evolved a lot. Its first stable release in November 2013 marked the point when it was the time to start taking it seriously in the production environment. Dart 1.9+ might, at first sight, look like what JavaScript could be if it was designed for today's Web. It combines the best of many other languages while targeting both browser and server-side development.

Dart isn't the answer to every problem on the Web. There are situations where it seems like it's overly complicated to use Dart or it just isn't good at what you need, and you might be right. There are circumstances where it's better to use JavaScript.

This book tries to be objective. We won't try to convince you that from now on, you should use only Dart, and we'll talk about situations where Dart isn't the ideal solution. At the same time, we'll show you where Dart is great, how you can write well-structured code for both the browser and the server, and how easy it is to write understandable asynchronous apps with Dart 1.9.

Even though this book can't go into great detail about each topic, after reading this book, you should see for yourself that Dart makes sense and you should at least give it a try. It's not just the language but also the IDE, comfortable debugger, dependency management, runtime profiler, and more.

What this book covers

Chapter 1, *Getting Started with Dart*, jumpstarts Dart development right away while explaining the syntax and core features of Dart.

Chapter 2, *Practical Dart*, focuses on the most common tasks of client-side development, such as DOM manipulation, asynchronous programming, Ajax calls, and using existing JavaScript code in Dart and vice versa.

Chapter 3, The Power of HTML5 with Dart, specifically focuses on using HTML5 features in Dart while mentioning some noteworthy third-party libraries written for Dart.

Chapter 4, Developing a Mobile App with Dart, builds on the previous chapter with a quick explanation of CSS3 transformations and HTML5 features specific for mobile devices.

Chapter 5, Web Components and polymer.dart, goes step by step, showing each part of Web Components standard and how useful they are, even when used separately. Then, it looks at polymer.dart, which combines all parts of Web Components into a single framework.

Chapter 6, AngularDart, is a sneak peak of a superheroic framework for Dart made by Google with the same philosophy in mind as AngularJS.

Chapter 7, Server-side Applications with Dart, shows that apart from the browser environment, there's also a standalone Dart VM, which can run on a server. We'll take a very practical look at writing server-side scripts, including server configuration for Apache and nginx web servers.

Chapter 8, Testing and Profiling the Dart Code, states that just as with any other language, unit testing is a vital part of the development process. Dart also comes with a built-in tool called Observer to examine Dart VM's internals in runtime.

Chapter 9, Writing Native Extensions for the Standalone Dart VM, shows the full potential of Dart, by writing native extensions for the standalone Dart VM in C/C++ and then using them from Dart.

What you need for this book

The only software you need is the Dart SDK. Right now, it's available for all recent releases of Windows, OS X, and Ubuntu Linux.

In *Chapter 9, Writing Native Extensions for the Standalone Dart VM*, we'll also need a C/C++ compiler, ideally GCC, which is free. This is actually optional; you don't need it if you don't want to try the examples for yourself.

Who this book is for

This book is intended for developers with prior knowledge of programming in any OOP language, with a reasonable background in web development and decent experience with JavaScript.

We're not going to go through basic programming constructs, such as conditionals, loops, boolean expressions, and similar things, which are common to all languages.

Also, we're not going to explain concepts of OOP.

Conventions

In this book, you will find a number of styles of text that distinguish between different kinds of information. Here are some examples of these styles, and an explanation of their meaning.

Code words in text, database table names, folder names, filenames, file extensions, pathnames, dummy URLs, user input, and Twitter handles are shown as follows: "The Reddit API allows us to set a custom callback with the jsonp parameter."

A block of code is set as follows:

```
import 'dart:html';
main() {
  print("Hello, world!");
}
```

When we wish to draw your attention to a particular part of a code block, the relevant lines or items are set in bold:

```
<input type="time" ng-model="newTask['when']">
<input type="text" ng-model="newTask['title']">
<button type="button"
    ng-click="addTask(newTask['when'], newTask['title'])">
Add</button>
```

Any command-line input or output is written as follows:

```
# dart bin/server.dart -p 8889
```

New terms and **important words** are shown in bold. Words that you see on the screen, in menus or dialog boxes for example, appear in the text like this: "In the **Emulation** tab, click on **Sensors** and you should see three input fields, each for one axis."

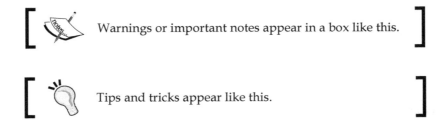

[Warnings or important notes appear in a box like this.]

[Tips and tricks appear like this.]

Reader feedback

Feedback from our readers is always welcome. Let us know what you think about this book—what you liked or may have disliked. Reader feedback is important for us to develop titles that you really get the most out of.

To send us general feedback, simply send an e-mail to feedback@packtpub.com, and mention the book title via the subject of your message.

If there is a topic that you have expertise in and you are interested in either writing or contributing to a book, see our author guide on www.packtpub.com/authors.

Customer support

Now that you are the proud owner of a Packt book, we have a number of things to help you to get the most from your purchase.

Downloading the example code

You can download the example code files for all Packt books you have purchased from your account at http://www.packtpub.com. If you purchased this book elsewhere, you can visit http://www.packtpub.com/support and register to have the files e-mailed directly to you.

Downloading the color images of this book

We also provide you with a PDF file that has color images of the screenshots/ diagrams used in this book. The color images will help you better understand the changes in the output. You can download this file from: `http://www.packtpub. com/sites/default/files/downloads/9607OS_GraphicsBundle.pdf`.

Errata

Although we have taken every care to ensure the accuracy of our content, mistakes do happen. If you find a mistake in one of our books — maybe a mistake in the text or the code — we would be grateful if you would report this to us. By doing so, you can save other readers from frustration and help us improve subsequent versions of this book. If you find any errata, please report them by visiting `http://www.packtpub. com/submit-errata`, selecting your book, clicking on the **errata submission form** link, and entering the details of your errata. Once your errata are verified, your submission will be accepted and the errata will be uploaded on our website, or added to any list of existing errata, under the Errata section of that title. Any existing errata can be viewed by selecting your title from `http://www.packtpub.com/support`.

Piracy

Piracy of copyright material on the Internet is an ongoing problem across all media. At Packt, we take the protection of our copyright and licenses very seriously. If you come across any illegal copies of our works, in any form, on the Internet, please provide us with the location address or website name immediately so that we can pursue a remedy.

Please contact us at `copyright@packtpub.com` with a link to the suspected pirated material.

We appreciate your help in protecting our authors, and our ability to bring you valuable content.

Questions

You can contact us at `questions@packtpub.com` if you are having a problem with any aspect of the book, and we will do our best to address it.

1
Getting Started with Dart

The first chapter will introduce us to the world of Dart. We'll learn:

- What is so interesting about Dart and why it's worth your time to give it a try
- Where and how to get the Dart SDK with its IDE called Dart Editor
- How to create the first app and see how to run and debug it in Dartium
- How to compile our app to JavaScript

What is Dart?

The Dart language was first unveiled at the *GOTO* conference in Aarhus in October 2011. Its primary goal, in the long run, is to replace JavaScript as the only language in browsers.

Although JavaScript is very easy to use for smaller apps, with the increasing complexity and the necessity to scale today's projects, it quickly becomes very hard to maintain. Frankly, JavaScript wasn't designed for this and writing larger apps is just a pain.

Dart was created as a brand new language with C-style syntax; it's object-oriented and class-based with a single inheritance model with mixins. It gives you many things that you've probably already used in other languages, such as abstract classes, encapsulation, reflection, exceptions, and so on. On the top of that, you can make use of optional static type checking.

Then, if you look a little deeper, you'll find things such as Future-Based API for all asynchronous calls, typedefs, isolates, streams, zones, dependency management, and even more out of the box. You'll probably find many of these things already familiar, but as you'll see, Dart uses a very easy-to-understand approach, which allows you to stay focused on writing your apps instead of dealing with the language itself.

In November 2013, Dart reached its first stable release, 1.0, and is still in active development.

On March 23, 2015, the Dart team released version 1.9, which significantly simplified working with asynchronous APIs and is considered the most important release since version 1.0.

At the end of April 2015, Google held the first Dart Summit revealing plans to use Dart as a language for cross-platform mobile development with their new runtime called **Fletch**.

Why choose Dart?

There are five main environments where you can run Dart:

- Dart compiled to JavaScript in practically any modern browser. The Dart SDK is shipped with Dart to a JavaScript compiler called `dart2js`, which takes your Dart code and compiles it into vanilla JavaScript. Right now, this is the most typical use case in a production environment.

- The Dartium web browser comes out of the box with the Dart SDK. It's a modified version of Chromium (basically, an open sourced Chrome) that contains Dart VM along with JavaScript V8. We'll use Dartium for easy debugging and to run the Dart code without compiling it to JavaScript.

- The standalone Dart VM allows you to run Dart code as a CLI script just like any other scripting language. The `dart2js` compiler itself is written in Dart.

- Google Cloud Platform, since the introduction of Google's Managed VMs in November 2014, it also supports a hosting environment for server-side code written in Dart.

- Fletch is an experimental highly concurrent Dart runtime, which will be able to run on both desktop and mobile platforms. It is scheduled for its official release at the end of 2015.

Dart VM is able to run your Dart code significantly more effectively than JavaScript V8. You can see current benchmarks at `www.dartlang.org/performance/`. Note that the `dart2js` compiler is doing pretty good even though the compilation process brings some additional overhead.

After the first public release of Dart, Google claimed they were planning to implement Dart VM right into Chrome as an alternative to JavaScript. However, on March 25, 2015, the Dart team released a blog post stating that after collecting reactions from their internal teams, they've decided to stop efforts to integrate Dart VM with Chrome and rather focus on improving integration with JavaScript.

Installing the Dart SDK

Let's start with obtaining the Dart SDK, which already contains all we need. This includes Dart Editor, the standalone Dart VM, and Dartium browser.

We can download everything in a single package right from Dart's home page at `https://www.dartlang.org/`, which detects your platform automatically for you and gives you the correct package for download.

Dart Editor

Dart Editor is built on the Eclipse platform, so you might find its look and feel already familiar.

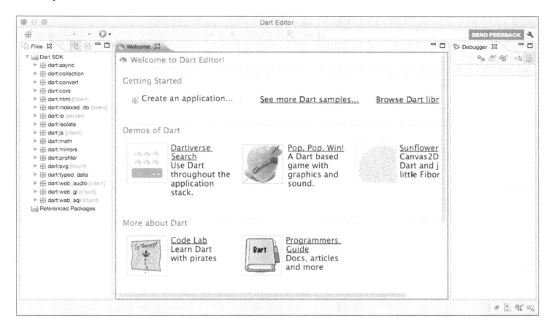

We're going to spend a lot of time in this editor, so feel free to take a look at it and try the example projects. This editor also contains a debugger that works out of the box with Dartium, so we don't need to configure anything.

Although the browser that comes with the Dart SDK package is actually called Chromium, we call it Dartium because it runs Dart VM inside. Even in Dart Editor, they call it Dartium, so don't be confused when you hit **Run in Dartium** and it opens the Chromium browser.

There's also a Dart plugin for IDEs developed by JetBrains, specifically, WebStorm, PHPStorm, and IntelliJ IDEA.

We're going to use Dart Editor in this book. However, the Dart team announced that they're planning to move to JetBrains IDEs and abandon Dart Editor probably in late 2015.

Writing a greeting for all Dartisans

Our first Dart app will randomly generate five colors in the `<ul>` element; let's enter a name into the `<input>` field and greet you with a selected color inside `<h1>`.

The final working app with some CSS will look like this:

We'll set off by creating a new project by clicking on **Create an application** in the Welcome window or by going to **File | New Project**. There are a few templates for the most common use cases. We'll go with Uber Simple Web Application because we need just the most basic app structure right now.

Our project should look like this:

For us, the most important files are `pubspec.yaml`, `index.html`, and `main.dart`. We can take a look at them one by one.

pubspec.yaml

This is a file that defines our project and its dependencies. By default, it contains only very basic information and one dependency called `browser`, which we'll use in `index.html`. If you're using Dart Editor, you can add more dependencies right in the editor's GUI, and you don't need to modify the file as text. Later in this chapter, we'll add more statements that control, for example, the `dart2js` compiler. For now, we can leave it as it is:

```
name: 'my_first_dart_app'
version: 0.0.1
description: An absolute bare-bones web app.
environment:
  sdk: '>=1.0.0 <2.0.0'
dependencies:
  browser: any
```

Note that dependencies in Dart projects don't necessarily need to contain any Dart code. For example, `browser` contains only two JavaScript files.

Downloading the example code

You can download the example code files from your account at
http://www.packtpub.com for all the Packt Publishing books
you have purchased. If you purchased this book elsewhere, you can
visit http://www.packtpub.com/support and register to have
the files e-mailed directly to you.

When you modify pubspec.yaml, Dart Editor downloads new dependencies
automatically for you.

We used any to specify the version for the browser package, which means that
the newest available version will be used. There are more ways to define allowed
versions; for a more detailed description, refer to https://www.dartlang.org/
tools/pub/dependencies.html. We'll use this option to set specific versions when
working with polymer.dart and AngularDart in *Chapter 5, Web Components and
polymer.dart*, and *Chapter 6, AngularDart*.

index.html

This is going to be just a simple HTML page:

```
<!DOCTYPE html>
<html>
<head>
  <meta charset="utf-8">
  <title>my_first_dart_app</title>
  <link rel="stylesheet" href="styles/main.css">
</head>

<body>
  <ul id="color-select"></ul>
  <input type="text" id="name">
  <h1 id="output"></h1>

  <script type="application/dart" src="main.dart"></script>
  <script data-pub-inline src="packages/browser/dart.js"></script>
</body>
</html>
```

Look at the last two `<script>` tags. The first one links the `main.dart` file, which is an entry point for our app. No matter how many files your Dart project has, you always link just the one that contains the `main()` function, as we'll see in a moment.

The `browser` package contains a script called `dart.js` that you'll probably use in all the Dart web projects you'll make. When you compile the Dart code to JavaScript, it creates a new file called `main.dart.js` with all your Dart code compiled to JavaScript. The `dart.js` script automatically checks whether your browser supports Dart natively and if it doesn't, it replaces `main.dart` with `dart.main.js`. Therefore, you can develop, test, and deploy projects in both Dart and JavaScript without even touching the HTML code. The `data-pub-inline` attribute tells the compiler to handle this element in a special way. We'll talk about this later in this chapter.

In this file, we created three elements (`<ul>`, `<h1>`, and `<input>`) that will be controlled from Dart.

 We're omitting the CSS file here and in most of the book as well, unless there's something particularly interesting and related to the topic. You can download all the source code for this book from the Packt Publishing website.

The main() function

The real fun starts here. The entry point to the app is the top-level `main()` function and as Dart is a class-based language, we'll create a class called `GreetingsManager` that will update the text and its color.

We can jump right into the code to get a quick glimpse of what Dart code looks like. Try to read the code and guess what you think it does. I believe that even without any knowledge of Dart, you'll be able to tell how it works.

```dart
// web/main.dart
import 'dart:html';
import 'dart:math';

class GreetingsManager {
  Random _rnd; // Random number generator.
  HtmlElement h1 = querySelector('#output');

  GreetingsManager() {
    _rnd = new Random();
  }
```

```dart
    // Generate a random color.
    String getRandomColor() {
      // Randomly generate numbers as hex strings with padding.
      return _rnd.nextInt(256).toRadixString(16).padLeft(2, '0') +
             _rnd.nextInt(256).toRadixString(16).padLeft(2, '0') +
             _rnd.nextInt(256).toRadixString(16).padLeft(2, '0');
    }


    // Generate a list of strings where each item represents one
    // color. [List<T>.generate()] is a named constructor that
    // calls the callback function n-times.
    List<String> generateColors(int total) {
      return new List<String>.generate(total, (int i) =>
          getRandomColor());
    }


    void setTextColor(String color) {
      SpanElement span = h1.querySelector('span');
      if (span != null) {
        span.style.color = color;
      }
    }


    void setText(String name) {
      // Override its inner HTML.
      h1.innerHtml = name.trim().isEmpty
          ? ""
          : "Hello, <span>$name</span>!";
    }
}

void main() {
  var gm = new GreetingsManager();

  // Target container for our colors.
  UListElement ul = querySelector('#color-select');

  // Iterate all colors and create <li> element for each of them.
  gm.generateColors(5).forEach((String color) {
    LIElement elm = new LIElement();
    // Set the background color.
    elm.style.backgroundColor = "#${color}";
```

```
    // Bind a listener to the onClick event.
    elm.onClick.listen((e) {
      gm.setTextColor(elm.style.backgroundColor);
      ul.querySelectorAll('li').classes.remove('selected');
      elm.classes.add('selected');
    });
    // Add HTML element to the <ul>.
    ul.append(elm);
  });

  InputElement nameInput = querySelector('#name');
  // Bind a listener to the onKeyUp event.
  nameInput.onKeyUp.listen((Event e) {
    String name = (e.target as InputElement).value;
    // print() outputs a variable as a string to
    // the environment's standard output.
    print(name);

    gm.setText(name);
    LIElement selected = ul.querySelector('li.selected');

    if (selected != null) {
      gm.setTextColor(selected.style.backgroundColor);
    }
  });
}
```

There are a couple of important things to pay attention to in more detail.

The code starts with `import` statements. These tell Dart to import (as you've probably guessed) another file or a package. Starting with `dart:`, it means that this is a built-in package that's shipped with the Dart SDK. Later, we'll also use `package:`, which is a third-party dependency, and at the end of the book, we'll meet `dart-ext:`, which is a native extension of the Dart VM. Of course, we'll use `import` to import files from our own projects as well.

All web apps will probably import the `dart:html` library because it makes top-level variables, `document` and `window`, and methods, such as `querySelector()` or `querySelectorAll()`, available.

Then, we declared a `GreetingsManager` class. If we didn't write a constructor for it, Dart would use the so-called implicit constructor by default. There's also a named constructor that we'll meet later.

All types in Dart are optional, but we're going to use them a lot in this book. It's not only easier to read; it also helps you spot possible errors and in some situations improves performance when compiled to JavaScript. If you don't care what type a variable is, you can declare it as var like in JavaScript, and the Dart static check won't bother you with it. There's also a special type dynamic, which is used underneath every time you don't specify a variable type, but in most situations, you're just fine with declaring variables with var. The dynamic keyword makes more sense when used as a generic keyword for List and Map classes, as we'll see later.

Every method in Dart has a return type, although you can use dynamic and void as well (omitting return type stands for void). Void means that this method doesn't return any value. Note that void doesn't have the same meaning as null. Null means zero or an undefined pointer, which is a valid value, while void means *nothing* in this context.

Collections such as lists are defined in Dart's API as List<E>. This means that the List class is generic and you can tell it what type of objects it may contain. In our example, we defined List<String>, which tells the type checker that all items in this collection will be instances of String. This notation of generics is very common in Java and C++, but as Dart types are optional, it actually doesn't restrict you from adding instances of other classes to the list, as you might expect. Using generics properly in Dart is a matter of a good programming style because it helps you and other developers understand your intentions. By the way, this is another situation where you can use the dynamic type if your list can contain any objects. As types are optional in Dart, declaring List<dynamic> is equal to not using the <E> notation at all. We'll see this in use later.

> Notice the way we access HTML element properties and how we can change their CSS style with elm.style.backgroundColor. Adding, removing, or toggling the classes of an element is very easy because the classes property is an instance of CssClassSet, which has many useful methods, and we can use elm.classes.add('selected'), for example. With Dart, most of the time, you don't need to access element attributes directly.

To remove element's classes, we can use querySelectorAll('li').classes. remove('selected'), where querySelectorAll() returns a collection of elements and performs .classes.remove('selected') on each of them. This approach is well known from jQuery, and it saves you a lot of writing the same code over and over again.

Then, we have the `main()` function, which is an entry point to our app. Dart VM parses your code before running it, so it doesn't matter where in the file you put it (it still has to be a top-level function). There, we call the `GreetingsManager.generateColors()` method and chain it with the `forEach()` method. All iterable collections implement the `forEach()` method, which calls a callback for each item in the collection. Creating an anonymous function has two possible formats. A short one-liner with just one expression, which we used in `generateColors()`, is as follows:

```
(int i) => getRandomColor()
```

This takes one parameter, calls `getRandomColor()`, and returns its result. This notation is equivalent to the second and is probably a more common format:

```
(int i) {
  return getRandomColor();
}
```

There is also another way we could iterate the entire collection:

```
for (String str in gm.generateColors()) {
  /* ... */
}
```

Listening to events is done via Dart streams, which is basically a way of handling asynchronous calls. For the most part, we can use them just like events in JavaScript. In our app, we're listening to the `onKeyUp` and `onClick` events. We "listen" to them by calling the `listen()` method that takes a callback function as an argument.

Dart lets you use type casting in a similar way to C/C++ with the `variable as type` notation (where `as` is a keyword). This is useful when the static checker doesn't know what type of object is stored in a variable but you know what you're expecting. We used it like `(e.target as InputElement).value` because we know that `e.target` is going to be of the `InputElement` type but `e.target` is a general `dynamic` property that doesn't have the `value` property itself. Of course, we could omit the typecast completely and just ignore the warning shown by type checker, but that's not a very good practice.

The last interesting thing is string interpolation. We can concatenate `String` objects in Dart with a plus sign +, but this tends to be confusing when used too much. Therefore, we can insert variables right into the string and leave Dart to do the work for us. In our app, we used it like this:

```
"Hello, <span>$name</span>!"
```

The $variable notations are replaced with a string representation of their variables. Interpolation can be used for expressions as well with ${expr}, for example, ${42. toString()}.

Running and debugging code in Dartium

Our code is done for now, so we can run the app in the browser. First, we'll test it in Dartium because it's able to run the native Dart code.

You can right-click on index.html and select **Run in Dartium**, or you can click on the white arrow in the green circle icon in the toolbar. This opens the Dartium browser and you should see the same page with five random colors just like what's shown at the beginning of this chapter. Open **Developer Tools** and see whether the browser really uses our main.dart file.

Debugging Dart scripts is very easy because we can use exactly the same tools used for debugging JavaScript. With Developer Tools, we can only debug web apps and not console apps.

Another way to debug both web and console apps is right in Dart Editor. Double-click on any line number to place a breakpoint and Dart VM will pause when it reaches that line.

Compiling Dart to JavaScript

From a practical point of view, Dart would be useless if we couldn't run it in today's browsers. This is why the Dart SDK comes with Dart to JavaScript compiler called `dart2js`. You can run it right in Dart Editor; in the top menu bar, navigate to **Tools | Pub Build** or right-click on `index.html` and select **Run as JavaScript**. This launches the compilation process and outputs some info:

```
--- 3:12:49 AM Running pub build on ./my_first_dart_app ... ---
Loading source assets...
Building my_first_dart_app...
[Info from Dart2JS]:
Compiling my_first_dart_app|web/main.dart...
[Info from Dart2JS]:
Took 0:00:07.294964 to compile my_first_dart_app|web/main.dart.
Built 224 files to "build".
```

As you can see, the compiler had to process 224 files in total and generated one large `main.dart.js` file, which we already mentioned earlier in this chapter. The compiler created a new directory named `build` and put there everything you need to run the app in both Dart and JavaScript.

You can run the compiler in CLI by navigating to your project's directory and running:

```
$ pub build
```

This command fetches all the dependencies, compiles your code with `dart2js`, and eventually processes it with transformers.

A very obvious question is how big the generated JavaScript file is. The Dart compiler removes parts of the code that your app isn't using and in Dart SDK 1.9, the final script is 290 KB. That's not bad but especially for mobile connections, it's still quite a lot. Luckily for us, we can tell `dart2js` to minify the final JavaScript by adding a new statement at the end of `pubspec.yaml` (you have to open the file as a text file or switch to the **Source** tab at the bottom of Dart Editor's window):

```
transformers:
- $dart2js:
    minify: true
```

When we run the compilation again, it will generate a 125 KB file. That's much better; keep in mind that this also includes all our project's code. For comparison, jQuery 2.1 that doesn't contain legacy code for older browsers and without our app code has 84 KB. With gzip compression enabled on your server, the difference is even smaller: 37 KB for `dart2js` versus 30 KB for jQuery. With the latest Dart Editor 1.9, you can create minimized version right from the **Tools** menu; however, setting it specifically in `pubspec.yaml` is sometimes necessary when using Dart's `pub` tool in CLI (more about this in the next chapter).

There's still one more thing to optimize. Our `index.html` includes JavaScript called `dart.js`, which we've already talked about. The template that we used has a special attribute, `data-pub-inline`:

```
<script data-pub-inline src="packages/browser/dart.js"></script>
```

By default, it does nothing. Let's add a new dependency to our project called `script_inliner` and then update `pubspec.yaml` again with:

```
transformers:
- $dart2js:
    minify: true
- script_inliner
```

Then, run **Pub Build** again; `script_inliner` processes HTML files and inlines JavaScripts marked as `data-pub-inline`.

The Dart language tour

We've already gone through many concepts of the Dart language when explaining the code, but there are still some aspects that we should look at in greater detail.

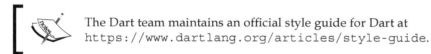 The Dart team maintains an official style guide for Dart at `https://www.dartlang.org/articles/style-guide`.

The static checker

Dart VM can run in **production** or **checked** mode. The checked mode performs runtime type checking and runs all `assert(condition)` checks. Asserts are a way to quickly test whether a condition is true, and if it's not, then stop the script execution. Runtime type checks can, for example, detect when you declare a variable `int` and then try to assign it a `String` object.

This is useful when developing or testing your app, but it introduces some overhead, and for this reason, Dart VM runs in production mode by default and simply ignores all these checks.

Dart Editor launches Dartium with enabled checked mode, but you can switch to production mode in the top menu window by navigating to **Run** | **Manage Launches** and by unchecking **Run in checked mode** for the configuration that runs in Dartium. For the standalone Dart VM, you can enable the checked mode with the `-c` parameter (for example, in command line, `dart -c main-cli.dart`).

Variables

We've already seen how to declare variables and we also saw that all types in Dart are optional. Apart from this, we can define variables as `const` or `final`.

The `final` keyword lets you assign a value to a variable only once. This behavior is slightly different when assigning objects because `final` only locks a variable's values and when you're assigning objects, you're working with pointers (their memory addresses). In other words, you're assigning a memory address to a variable and it doesn't care what the internal state of the object is. It can change in runtime. The `final` keyword only prevents you from assigning a different value to the same variable. For example, you can declare an instance of `List<String>` as `final` and add items dynamically during the app's lifetime.

The `const` keyword lets you assign a value to a variable at compile time. For this reason, you can't make a variable `const` if its value is dependent on an expression that isn't determinable at compile time. The same restrictions are applied when instantiating objects where all their properties have to be compile time determinable too.

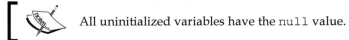 All uninitialized variables have the `null` value.

Built-in types

Everything in Dart is an object; however, some types are treated in a special way:

- **Numbers**: Built-in `int` and `double` types are both subclasses of the `num` abstract class. All integers and floating point numbers are stored as `int` or `double`, respectively.

- **Strings**: All strings in Dart are stored as `String` objects. Both single and double quotes to enclose a string are allowed. Classes can implement the `toString()` method, which should return a textual representation of the inner state of an object.

- **Booleans**: These are `true`/`false` values. Note that in JavaScript, a value is considered to be true if it's a nonzero length string, nonempty array, any value different from 0, and so on. But in Dart, *only the Boolean value* `true` *is treated as true*, nothing else.

- **Lists**: All lists (or arrays) are instances of `List` class. You can use short notations to create lists just like in JavaScript with this:
  ```
  List<T> list = [1, 2, 3];
  ```

- **Maps**: Key-value storage in Dart is represented by the `Map` class. You can use short notation with this as well:

```
Map<K,V> map = {
   'key1' => 'value',
   'key2' => 123
};
```

You can get a value associated to a key with a square bracket notation, such as `map['key']`. In contrast to JavaScript, the `Map` class in Dart has a public property, `length`, which represents the total number of key-value pairs in the map.

Functions and parameters

Defining functions is nothing new, and we've already seen this in the preceding sections. Dart extends function definitions with optional positional and named parameters, both well known from Python.

After the required parameters, you can specify any number of optional parameters.

Named parameters are mostly useful when you have a function with many parameters, and in most use cases, you need to use only a few of them. You can define named parameters as a map with curly brackets, `{}`:

```
void myFunc(required, {bool opt1: true, String opt2: "hello"}) {
   /* ... */
}
```

Another method is to use optional positional parameters. You can define positional parameters with square brackets, `[]`:

```
void myFunc2(required, [bool named1, String named2]) {
   /* ... */
}
```

One function definition *can't combine both* named and positional optional parameters. Some examples of calling both types could be:

```
myFunc(true, opt2: "Hello, World!");
myFunc2(false, true, "I'm Dart");
```

Class properties

When defining classes, there are no `public`, `protected` or `private` keywords like in PHP or Java. Instead, every property that starts with _ is private. Everything else is public. Dart also generates default getters and setters for each property, but you can override them or create your custom properties:

```
Class Square {
  num height;
  num width;

  num get size => height * width;
  set size(int value) {
    width = height = sqrt(value);
  }
}
```

You can later use `size` just like any other public property:

```
var cls = new Square();
cls.size = 49;
```

This updates both `width` and `height`.

Class inheritance and abstract classes

Dart is an object-oriented language with a mixin-based inheritance model. This means that every class has exactly one superclass but can implement multiple classes as interfaces and use multiple class bodies (mixins). Every class is at least a subclass of the `Object` class.

Abstract classes can't be instantiated directly and often contain abstract methods.

Any class in Dart can be treated as an interface for another class, which might be a little unusual:

```
abstract class MyAbsClass {
  String hello();
}
class MyInterface {
  String hello2() => "hello!";
}
class MyInterface2 {
  String anotherHello() => "hello!";
}
```

```
class MyClass extends MyAbsClass implements MyInterface, MyInterface2
{
  String hello() => "Ahoy";
  String hello2() {
    /* ... */
  }
  String anotherHello() {
    /* ... */
  }
}
```

Note that the `hello()` abstract method in `MyAbsClass` doesn't need a keyword in front of it. It just doesn't have any body. The `MyClass` class implements two classes as its interfaces and automatically takes all their methods as abstract and requires you to implement them. This isn't the same as inheritance because it completely ignores methods' bodies and expects you to write them by yourself. There's also keyword `super` that refers to the superclass.

In later chapters, we'll explain and use mixins as well.

Constructors

There are two types of constructors, **generative** and **named**. Generative constructors are the same constructors as in any other language. Their name equals the class name:

```
class MyClassWithConst {
  num height;
  num width;

  MyClassWithConst(num w, num h) {
    width = w;
    height = h;
  }
}
```

Assigning default values to object properties is very common, so there's a shorter way to write the preceding constructor with just the following:

```
MyClassWithConst(this.width, this.height);
```

Since there's no constructor overloading (like in Java or C++), Dart offers named constructors:

```
class MyClassWithConst {
  /* ... */
  MyClassWithConst(this.width, this.height);

  MyClassWithConst.withZeros() {
    this.width = 0;
    this.height = 0;
  }
}
```

Note that constructors aren't inherited from superclasses and you don't even have to define any constructor and Dart will use a default one for you (just the class name with no parameters).

Exceptions

Dart supports throwing exceptions when something goes wrong. The logic behind this is just like in any other language, so it probably doesn't require any further explanation:

```
throw new Exception("It's broken");
```

Catching exceptions is based on typical `try`, `catch`, and `final` statements. You can catch only specific exceptions or make general `catch` statements for all exceptions:

```
try {
  brokenFunction();
} on MyOwnException {
  itsNotThatBad();
} catch (e) { //
  itsPrettyBad();
} finally {
  cleanup();
}
```

Custom defined exceptions have to inherit from the `Exception` class.

Using static types

It might look like it's better to always specify variable types everywhere. The rule of thumb here is to use types when it's unclear what the variable type is, including return types. For example, look at the following code:

```
GreetingsManager gm = new GreetingsManager();
```

Instead of writing the class name twice, we use the following:

```
var gm = new GreetingsManager();
```

The static analyzer knows that the gm variable is assigned to a GreetingsManager class, so it's fine to use just var. This also applies when iterating collections:

```
List<String> colors = ['red', 'green', 'blue'];
for (var color in colors) { }
```

We don't need to declare String color because this is obvious from the List<String> declaration.

The same approach is recommended when using void and dynamic. If there's no good reason to specify them, just omit them.

Summary

This is probably enough for the first chapter. There're still topics to be covered and we'll explain more Dart concepts in later chapters when we come across them.

You can see that Dart uses a lot of ideas from other languages and that it requires very little knowledge to be able to start using it.

In the next chapter, we'll write another app that uses a lot of the stuff that we learned now. We'll also take a look at using existing JavaScript code in Dart and vice versa, which is a very interesting and practical topic for every Dart learner. For easier migration from other languages to Dart, you can take a look at the list of synonyms in Dart and other languages at https://www.dartlang.org/docs/synonyms/.

2
Practical Dart

This chapter will focus on the most common features of Dart that you'll use every day for your next Dart project. In this chapter, we'll look at:

- Manipulating DOM and HTML elements
- Future-Based API, Dart's built-in library for working with asynchronous calls
- Creating Ajax requests in Dart
- How packages work in Dart
- Calling JavaScript from Dart
- Calling Dart from JavaScript

The whole chapter is intended to be very practical. We'll create a small app that reads a JSON dictionary and lets you search among all the terms in it. To make it more complicated, we'll implement a so-called fuzzy search algorithm, which doesn't search exact matches but the same order of characters instead.

Optimizing DOM tree manipulations

We've already seen some basic manipulation with HTML elements in *Chapter 1, Getting Started with Dart*, and we'll make a few notes about it here.

The Dart library wraps standard JavaScript element classes and methods with more unified names. Classes that represent HTML elements don t start with the `HTML` prefix, so for example, `HTMLDivElement` is called `DivElement` in Dart. Take a look at this JavaScript snippet:

```
elm.addEventListener('client', function() { /* ... */ });
```

Instead of binding event listeners with the preceding code, Dart uses the so-called **Stream API,** where you don't bind listeners directly to the element you subscribe but to a `Stream` object instead, which emits all events. Each HTML element has all the default event emitters, such as `onClick` or `onKeyPress`:

```
elm.onClick.listen((e) { /* ... */ });
```

The `listen()` method returns a `StreamSubscription` object that can be used to unsubscribe the listener.

Streams have many methods that you probably won't use so often, but take a look at Dart's API for what's available. One of these methods is the `where()` method, which is declared as:

```
Stream<T> where(Function bool test(T event));
```

Typical usage could be, for example:

```
document.onClick.where((Event e) => e.target.id == 'myButton');
```

This method creates a new `Stream` object that only emits events that pass the test function. This is useful, for example, when you only want to listen to a small subset of events that can be emitted by this listener. For example, you want to use `onClick` on the entire document and create special streams when the user clicks on a `<div>` element and another stream for `<p>` elements. Without `where()`, you would have to use one callback for all `onClick` events. With `where()`, you can make separate streams that let you or other developers bind specifically to them.

Another useful feature of the DOM is **DocumentFragment.** Manipulating with a lot of HTML elements, such as appending, removing, resizing, changing text content, and basically, any operation that visually changes the page, causes the browser to create "reflow". This is a browser procedure that recalculates the position of all the elements on the page in order to re-render the page.

In practice, you usually don't need to deal with this, but pages that contain thousands, or tens of thousands, of elements can be unresponsive for a short time. A good way to optimize this is to make changes to the DOM in bulks. For example, it's not recommended that you do this:

```
UlistElement cont = querySelector('#hello-ul');
cont.children.clear();
list.forEach((String key) {
    LIElement li = new LIElement();
    li.text = key;
    cont.append(li);
});
```

Each call to `append()` will make the browser run the reflow. However, browsers are well optimized these days and they would probably run just one reflow at the end because none of the statements in the `forEach()` loop need to work with positions or sizes. Try to add just a single innocent statement that does nothing right after `cont.append(li);` such as `cont.scrollTop;`. We know that appending `<li>` elements shouldn't change its `scrollTop` property but the browser doesn't know this and it has to do a reflow for every element in the list. We can analyze this in Dartium with Developer Tools in the **Timeline** tab.

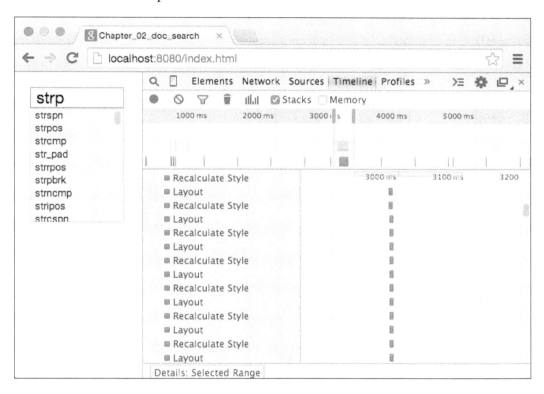

This is a sneak peak from the app we'll create in this chapter. Appending 346 elements took about 150 ms. This applies even when the parent element is hidden.

There's a better way to do this with `DocumentFragments`:

```
UlistElement cont = querySelector('#hello-ul');
var frag = new DocumentFragment();
list.forEach((String key) {
    LIElement li = new LIElement();
```

```
        li.text = key;
        frag.append(li);
    });
    cont.children.clear();
    cont.append(frag.clone(true));
```

This code has the same functionality as the previous but this time, we create `DocumentFragment`, which is a DOM tree itself but is not placed in the document. We add multiple elements to it and then append its entire content to the `<ul>` element. Take a look at the following screenshot:

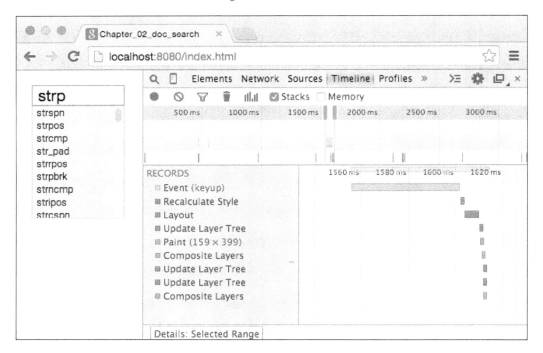

With `DocumentFragment`, creating and appending 346 elements took about 50 ms because it took just one reflow and spent most of the time by creating new instances of `LIElement`. Note that the Dartium browser works with the Dart code and events just like Chrome works with JavaScript. At first sight, you wouldn't even notice that the browser wasn't interpreting JavaScript.

The caveat here is that most of the time, we use third-party libraries and we have no idea what's going on inside them, so you can't rely on the browser's prediction whether or not it should run the reflow. `DocumentFragments` aren't new to HTML but at the same time, they aren't used by many developers even when their usage is very simple.

A common usage is also when you already have an existing DOM subtree that you want to modify multiple times. You can clone just the small subtree to `DocumentFragment`, modify it, and replace the original subtree.

Rules for minimizing reflows apply to everything that needs to work with position or size. Another example could be:

```
innerElement.style.width = '100px';
print(cont.clientWidth);
innerElement.style.height = '200px';
print(cont.clientHeight);
```

This calls two reflows because you set the width first and then access some elements' size, which causes the first reflow, and then the same for height, which causes the second reflow. We can rewrite this as the following, which creates just one reflow:

```
innerElement.style.width = '100px';
innerElement.style.height = '200px';
print(cont.clientWidth);
print(cont.clientHeight);
```

We'll see both the Stream API and document fragments in action right now.

The documentation search app

We're going to write an app that can search among many terms and show some simple detail for each of them. The search input field will have an autocomplete feature with a list of all the terms that match our search string.

Particularly, we'll use the documentation for PHP with 9,047 functions and write a fuzzy search algorithm that will search in it.

Fuzzy search is used in IDEs such as **PHPStorm** or **PyCharm** and also in the popular text editor **Sublime Text**. It doesn't search just for the strings that start with your search term but it checks whether the order of characters in your term and in the checked string is the same. For example, if you type `docfrg`, it will find `DocumentFragment` because the letters in `DocumentFragment` are in the same order as `docfrg`.

This is very handy because when there are a lot of functions with the same prefix, you can start typing with just the first character and then jump to the middle of the word and it's very likely that there won't be many functions with the same characters. This is quite common for PHP because there are a lot of functions that start with `mysql` or `str_`. If you're looking for a function called `str_replace`, you can type just `splc`.

We'll load the entire dictionary with Ajax as a JSON string and decode it to a `Map` object. Dart uses the Future-Based API for all asynchronous calls including Ajax, so we should talk about it first.

The Future-Based API

Dart, as well as JavaScript, uses asynchronous calls a lot. A common pitfall of this approach in JavaScript is that it tends to make many nested function calls with callbacks:

```
async1(function() {
  // do something
  async2(function() {
    // do something
    async3(function() {
      // do something
      callback();
    });
  }, callback);
});
```

The downsides of this approach are obvious:

- It makes hard to read and debug code, so-called **callback hell**.
- Each nested function can access variables from all parent scopes. This leads to **variable shadowing** and also prevents the JavaScript interpreter from deallocating unused variables. When working with a larger amount of data (for example, asynchronous calls when reading files), even simple script can use the entire available memory and cause the browser to crash.

A `Future` in Dart stands for an object that represents a value that will exist sometime in the future. Dart uses `Future` objects in nearly all their APIs, and we're going to use it in order to avoid passing callbacks around.

An example of using `Future` is `HttpRequest.getString()`, which returns a `Future` object immediately and makes an asynchronous Ajax call:

```
HttpRequest.getString('http://...').then(onDataReady);
```

To work with the data returned from a `Future` object, we use the `then()` method, which takes the callback function as an argument that can return another `Future` object as well.

If we want to create asynchronous behavior similar to that in the preceding example, we use the `Completer` class, which is a part of `dart:async` package. This class has a property called `future`, which represents our `Future` object and the `complete()` method, which resolves the `Future` object with some value. To keep the same order of function calls, we'll chain the `then()` methods of each `Future` object:

```
import 'dart:async';

Future async1() {
  var completer = new Completer();
  // Simulate long lasting async operation.
  new Future.delayed(const Duration(seconds: 2), () {
    // Resolve completer.future with this value. This will also
    // call callback passed to then() method for this Future.
    completer.complete('delayed call #1');
  });
  // Call to [Completer.complete()] resolves the Future object.
  return completer.future;
}

Future async2(String val) {
  // Print result from the previous async call.
  print(val);
  // Then create a new Completer and schedule
  // it for later execution.
  var completer = new Completer();
  // Simulate long lasting async operation.
  new Future.delayed(const Duration(seconds: 3), () {
    completer.complete('delayed call #2');
  });
  return completer.future;
}

Future async3(String val) {
  // Return another Future object.
}

void main() {
  // Chain async calls. Each function returns a Future object.
  async1()
    .then((String val) => async2(val))
    .then((String val) => async3(val))
    .then((String val) => print(val));
}
```

We got rid of nested calls and have quite straightforward, shallow code.

 APIs similar to Dart's `Future` are very common among most JavaScript frameworks. Maybe you've already seen `$.Deferred()` in jQuery or `$q.defer()` in AngularJS.

`Future` objects can also handle error states with `catchError()` that are emitted by a `Completer` object with `completeError()`.

Another usage of `Future` is when we want a function to be called asynchronously, which is internally scheduled at the end of the event queue:

```
new Future(() {
  // function body
});
```

Sometimes, this is useful when you want to let the browser process all the events before executing more computationally intensive tasks that could make the browser unresponsive for a moment. For more in-depth information about Dart's event loop, see `https://www.dartlang.org/articles/event-loop/`.

Using async and await keywords

Dart 1.9 introduced two new keywords, `async` and `await`, that significantly simplify the usage of asynchronous calls with the Future-Based API.

Async

The `async` keyword is used to mark a function's body (which immediately returns a `Future` object) that is executed later and its return value is used to complete the `Future` object just like we saw previously when using the `Completer` class:

```
Future<String> hello() async {
  return 'Hello, World!';
}
```

In practice, you don't have to specify the `Future<String>` return type because even Dart Editor knows that the `async` function returns a `Future` object, so we'll omit it most of the time.

This saves some writing but its real power comes in combination with `await`.

Await

With `Future` objects, the only way to chain (or simulate synchronous) calls is to use the `then()` method multiple times, as we saw earlier. But there's a new keyword `await` that is able to pause the execution of the current VM's thread and wait until the `Future` object is completed:

```
String greetings = await hello();
```

The completed value of `Future` is then used as a value for the entire expression `await hello()`.

In comparison to the preceding example of multiple asynchronous calls, we could use just:

```
print(await async3(await async2(await async1())));
```

The only limitation here is that `await` must be used inside an asynchronous function (for example, defined with `async`) in order not to block the main execution thread. If the expression with `await` raises an exception, it's propagated to its caller.

We're going to use `async` and `await` a lot here, but it's good to know how to use the "original" Future-Based API with the `Future` and `Complete` classes, because it will take some time for developers of third-party libraries to update their code with `async` and `await`.

 Dart 1.9 actually introduced even more keywords such as `await-for`, `yield`, `async*`, and a few more (also called **generators**), but these aren't very common and we're not going to discuss them here. If you want to know more about them, refer to `https://www.dartlang.org/articles/beyond-async/`.

Creating Ajax requests in Dart

Nearly every app these days uses Ajax. With libraries such as jQuery, it's very easy to make Ajax calls, and Dart is no different. Well, maybe the only difference is that Dart uses the Future-Based API.

Creating an Ajax call and getting the response is this easy:

```
String url = 'http://domain.com/foo/bar';
Future ajax = HttpRequest.getString(url);
ajax.then((String response) {
  print(response);
});
```

```
// Or even easier with await.
// Let's assume we're inside an asynchronous function.
String response = await HttpRequest.getString(url);
```

That's all. `HttpRequest.getString()` is a static method that returns a `Future<String>` object. When the response is ready, the callback function is called with the response as a string. You can handle an error state with `catchError()` method or just wrap the `await` expression with the `try-catch` block. By default, `getString()` uses the HTTP GET method.

There are also more general static methods such as `HttpRequest.request()`, which returns `Future<HttpRequest>`, where you can access return code, response type, and so on. Also, you can set a different HTTP method if you want.

To send form data via the POST method, the best way is to use `HttpRequest.postFormData()`, which takes a URL and a `Map` object with form fields as arguments.

In this chapter, we'll use Ajax to load a dictionary as JSON for our search algorithm, and we'll also see JSONP in action later.

Dart packages

Every Dart project that contains the `pubspec.yaml` file is also a package. Our search algorithm is a nice example of a component that can be used in multiple projects, so we'll stick to a few conventions that will make our code reusable.

Dart doesn't have namespaces like other languages, such as PHP, Java, or C++. Instead, it has libraries that are very similar in concept.

We'll start writing our app by creating a new project with the `Uber Simple Web Application` template and creating two directories. First, we create `/lib` in the project's root. Files in this directory are automatically made public for anyone using our package. The second directory is `/lib/src`, where we'll put the implementation of our library, which is going to be private. Let's create a new file in `/lib/fuzzy.dart`:

```
// lib/fuzzy.dart
library fuzzy;
part 'src/fuzzy_search.dart';
```

This creates a library called `fuzzy`. We could put all the code for this library right into `fuzzy.dart`, but that would be a mess. We'd rather split the implementation into multiple files and use the `part` keyword to tell Dart to make all the functions and classes defined in `lib/src/fuzzy_search.dart` public. One library can use the `part` keyword multiple times. Similarly to object properties, everything that starts with the _ underscore is private and not available from the outside.

Then, in `lib/src/fuzzy_search.dart`, we'll put just the basic skeleton code right now:

```
// lib/src/fuzzy_search.dart
part of fuzzy;
class FuzzySearch {
  /* ... */
}
```

The `part of` keyword tells Dart that this file belongs to the `fuzzy` library.

Then, in `main.dart`, we need to import our own library to be able to use the `FuzzySearch` class:

```
// web/main.dart
import 'package:Chapter_02_doc_search/fuzzy.dart';
// ... later in the code create an instance of FuzzySearch.
var obj = new FuzzySearch();
```

Note that the `fuzzy.dart` file is inside the `lib` directory, but we didn't have to specify it. The package importer is actually not working with directory names but package names, so `Chapter_02_doc_search` here is a package name from `pubspec.yaml` and not a directory, although these two have the same name. For more in-depth information about `pubspec.yaml` files, refer to `https://www.dartlang.org/tools/pub/pubspec.html`.

You should end up with a structure like this:

Note that the package has a reference to itself in the `packages` directory.

One package can be a library and a web app at the same time. If you think about it, it's not total nonsense, because you can create a library and ship it with a demo app that shows what the library does and how to use it.

 You can read more about Dart packages at `https://www.dartlang.org/tools/pub/package-layout.html`.

Writing the fuzzy search algorithm

We can move on with writing the fuzzy search algorithm. A proper name for this algorithm would be probably **approximate string matching**, because our implementation is simpler than the canonical and we don't handle typos. Try to read the code; we've already seen every language concept used here in *Chapter 1, Getting Started with Dart*:

```dart
// lib/src/fuzzy_search.dart
part of fuzzy;

class FuzzySearch {
  List<String> list;

  FuzzySearch(this.list);

  List<String> search(String term) {
    List<String> results = [];

    if (term.isEmpty) {
      return [];
    }

    // Iterate entire list.
    List<String> result = list.where((String key) {
      int ti = 0; // term index
      int si = 0; // key index
      // Check order of characters in the search
      // term and in the string key.
      for (int si = 0; si < key.length; si++) {
        if (term[ti] == key[si]) {
          ti++;
          if (ti == term.length) {
            return true;
          }
        }
      }
      return false;
    }).toList(growable: false);

    // Custom sort function.
    // We want the shorter terms to be first because it's more
    // likely that what you're looking for is there.
```

```
    result.sort((String a, String b) {
      if (a.length > b.length) {
        return 1;
      } else if (a.length == b.length) {
        return 0;
      }
      return -1;
    });

    return result;
  }
}
```

The app itself will require a simple HTML code (we're omitting obvious surrounding code, such as `<html>` or `<head>`):

```
<body>
  <input type="search" id="search" disabled>
  <ul id="autocomplete-results"></ul>

  <div id="detail">
    <h1></h1>
    <div></div>
  </div>

  <script type="application/dart" src="main.dart"></script>
  <script data-pub-inline src="packages/browser/dart.js"></script>
</body>
```

We don't want to hardcode the dictionary, so we'll load it using Ajax. JSON file with all search terms is part of this chapter's source code, and it looks like this:

```
{ ...
  "strpos": {
    "desc": "Find the numeric position of the first occurrence
      of 'needle' in the 'haystack' string.",
    "name": "strpos"
  },
    ...
  "pdo::commit": {
```

```
      "desc": "...",
      "name": "PDO::commit"
    }, ...
}
```

The key for each item is its lowercased name. In Dart, this JSON will be represented as:

```
Map<String, Map<String, String>>
```

Now, we'll write a static method that creates an instance of our app and the `main()` function:

```dart
import 'dart:html';
import 'dart:convert';
import 'dart:async';
import 'package:Chapter_02_doc_search/fuzzy.dart';

class DocSearch {
  static fromJson(Element root, String url) async {
    String json = await HttpRequest.getString(url);
    Map decoded = JSON.decode(json);
    return new DocSearch(root, decoded);
  }

  DocSearch(Element root, [Map<String, dynamic> inputDict]) {
    // Rest of the constructor.
  }
  // The rest of the class goes here.
}


main() async {
  try {
    await DocSearch.fromJson(querySelector('body'), 'dict.json');
  } catch(e) {
    print("It's broken.");
  }
}
```

Note how we're creating an instance of DocSearch and are declaring main() as asynchronous. We call a DocSearch.fromJson() static method, which returns a Future object (the async keyword does this for us automatically), which is completed with an instance of DocSearch when the Ajax call is finished and when we decoded JSON into a Map object.

 The source code for this example contains both Dart 1.9 implementation with async and await and pre 1.9 version with the raw Future and Completer classes.

Handling HTML elements

You can see that if we hardcoded our dictionary, we could call the constructor of DocSearch like with any other class. We can now look at the constructor particularly:

```
// web/main.dart
class DocSearch {
  Element _root;
  InputElement _input;
  UListElement _ul;
  FuzzySearch _fuzzy;
  Map<String, dynamic> _dict;

  static Future fromJson(Element root, String url) async {
    /* The same as above. */
  }

  DocSearch(Element root, [Map<String, dynamic> inputDict]) {
    _root = root;
    dict = inputDict;
    _input = _root.querySelector('input');
    _ul = _root.querySelector('ul');

    // Usage of ".." notation.
    _input
      ..attributes.remove('disabled')
      ..onKeyUp.listen((_) => search(_input.value))
      ..onFocus.listen((_) => showAutocomplete());

    _ul.onClick.listen((Event e) {
```

```
      Element target = e.target;
      showDetail(target.dataset['key']);
    });

    // Pass only clicks that are not into <ul> or <input>.
    Stream customOnClick = document.onClick.where((Event e) {
      Element target = e.target;
      return target != _input && target.parent != _ul;
    });
    customOnClick.listen((Event e) => hideAutocomplete());
  }


  /* The rest of the class goes here. */
}
```

To set multiple properties to the same object, we can use the **double dot** operator. This lets you avoid copying and pasting the same object name over and over again. This notation is equal to:

```
_input.attributes.remove('disabled')
_input.onKeyUp.listen((_) => search(_input.value))
_input.onFocus.listen((_) => showAutocomplete());
```

Of course, we can use it for more nested properties as well:

```
elm.attributes
  ..remove('whatever')
  ..putIfAbsent('value', 'key')
```

In the constructor, we're creating a custom `Stream` object, as we talked about earlier in this chapter. This stream passes only clicks outside our `<ul>` and `<input>` elements, which represent autocomplete container and a search input filed, respectively. We need to do this because we want to be able to hide the autocomplete when the user clicks outside of the search field. Using just `onBlur` in the input field (the lost focus event) wouldn't work as we wanted, because any click in the autocomplete would hide it immediately without emitting `onClick` inside the autocomplete.

This is a nice place for custom streams. We could also make our stream a public property and let other developers bind listeners to it. In vanilla JavaScript, you would probably do this as an event that checks both conditions and emits a second event and then listen only to the second event.

The rest of the code is mostly what we've already seen, but it's probably good idea to recap it in context. From now on, we'll skip obvious things such as DOM manipulation unless there's something important. We're also omitting CSS files because they aren't important to us:

```dart
// web/main.dart
class DocSearch {
  /* Properties are the same as above. */
  static fromJson(Element root, String url) async { /* ... */ }

  DocSearch(Element root, [Map<String, dynamic> inputDict]) {
    /* ... */
  }

  // Custom setter for dict property. When we change
  // the dictionary that this app uses, it will also change
  // the search list for the FuzzySearch instance.
  void set dict(Map<String, dynamic> dict) {
    _dict = dict;
    if (_fuzzy == null) {
      _fuzzy = new FuzzySearch(_dict.keys.toList());
    } else {
      _fuzzy.list = _dict.keys.toList();
    }
  }

  void search(String term) {
    if (term.length > 1) {
      int start = new DateTime.now().millisecondsSinceEpoch;
      List<String> results =
          _fuzzy.search(_input.value.toLowerCase());
      int end = new DateTime.now().millisecondsSinceEpoch;
      // Debug performance. Note the usage of interpolation.
      print('$term: ${(end - start).toString()} ms');

      renderAutocomplete(results);
    } else {
      hideAutocomplete();
    }
  }
}
```

```dart
    void renderAutocomplete(List<String> list) {
      if (list.length == 0) hideAutocomplete();
      // We'll use DocumentFragment as we talked about earlier.
      // http://jsperf.com/document-fragment-test-peluchetti
      DocumentFragment frag = new DocumentFragment();

      list.forEach((String key) {
        LIElement li = new LIElement();
        li.text = _dict[key]['name'];
        // Same as creating 'data-key' attribute or using data()
        // method in jQuery.
        li.dataset['key'] = key;
        frag.append(li);
      });

      _ul.children.clear();
      _ul.append(frag.clone(true));
      showAutocomplete();
    }

  void showDetail(String key) {
    Map<String, String> info = _dict[key];
    _root.querySelector('#detail > h1').text = info['name'];

    String desc = info['desc']
      ..replaceAll('\\n\\n', '</p><p>')
      ..replaceAll('\\_', '_');
    _root.querySelector('#detail > div').innerHtml =
        '<p>' + desc + '</p>';

    hideAutocomplete();
  }

  void showAutocomplete() { _ul.style.display = 'block'; }
  void hideAutocomplete() { _ul.style.display = 'none'; }
}
```

Note that we defined a custom setter for the `dict` property, so when we change it from anywhere in the code, it also changes the `list` property in the instance of the `FuzzySearch` class. Dart allows writing both custom getters and setters:

```
void set property(<T> newValue) {
  // Custom logic here.
}
<T> get property {
  // Custom logic here.
  // return an instance of <T>
}
```

Finally, we can test it in the browser:

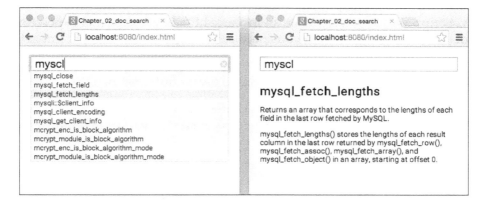

When you type at least two characters in the search field, it opens an autocomplete with suggested function names. You can click on one of them; it closes the autocomplete and shows a simple detail window with its name and description.

You can open Developer Tools and see how much time it took for Dart to traverse the entire 9,047 string list (it's about 25 ms on Intel Core Duo 2.5 GHz).

As we're already creating the `FuzzySearch` class as a reusable library, it would be nice if we could use it not just in Dart but also in JavaScript.

Combining Dart and JavaScript

Using Dart in JavaScript and JavaScript in Dart is very easy, although there are some limitations right now that will hopefully be resolved in the future. Basically, when exchanging data between JavaScript and Dart, all you have to do is to wrap/unwrap Dart objects with `JsArray`, `JsFunction`, or `JsObject` proxy classes from the `dart:js` built-in package.

Some built-in types don't need any proxy wrapper. The most common are `null`, `bool`, `num`, `String`, `DateTime`, `HtmlCollection`, `Event`, `Node`, and `NodeList`.

 Maybe you've already seen somebody using a `package:js/js.dart` package. This is the old Dart-JS interoperation package, which is deprecated in favor of `dart:js`.

Using Dart in JavaScript

Let's say we're writing a JavaScript app where we want to reuse our existing `FuzzySearch` class and print all results to the console.

As of now, we *can't* just expose the class definition and then create instances of it in JavaScript. We *can't* even create an instance of `FuzzySearch` and expose the entire object to JavaScript, where you could call `FuzzySearch.search()` or set `FuzzySearch.list` by yourself.

We need to wrap all calls to Dart into exposed JavaScript functions.

Create three files in the `web` directory: `test_fuzzy.dart`, `test_fuzzy.js`, and `test_fuzzy.html`. We'll start with `test_fuzzy.html` (again, we're omitting the unnecessary code):

```
<!-- web/test_fuzzy.html -->
<body>
  <script type="application/dart" src="test_fuzzy.dart"></script>
  <script data-pub-inline src="packages/browser/dart.js"></script>
  <script src="test_fuzzy.js"></script>
</body>
```

We still need some Dart code in the `main()` function that exposes what we want even when there's no app logic in it. Then add the following in `test_fuzzy.dart`:

```
// web/test_fuzzy.dart
import 'dart:js';
import 'package:Chapter_02_doc_search/fuzzy.dart';

void main() {
  FuzzySearch fuzzy = new FuzzySearch();

  context['dart_fuzzy_set_list'] = (JsArray array) {
    fuzzy.list = array.toList();
  };
  context['dart_fuzzy_search'] = fuzzy.search;
}
```

The top-level `context` variable comes from the `dart:js` package. You can think of it as the `window` object in JavaScript. We create two functions:

- `dart_fuzzy_set_list()`: This takes a JavaScript array as an argument, creates a `List` object from it, and passes it to our instance of `FuzzySearch`

- `dart_fuzzy_search()`: This just exposes `FuzzySearch.search()` for this instance

Then, in `test_fuzzy.js`, we use vanilla JavaScript:

```
// web/test_fuzzy.js
window.onload = function() {
  var terms =
    ['strpos', 'str_replace', 'strrev', 'substr', 'strtotime'];
  window.dart_fuzzy_set_list(terms);

  var results = window.dart_fuzzy_search('srr');
  console.log(results);

  for (var i = 0; i < results.o.length; i++) {
    console.log(results.o[i]);
  }
};
```

That's it. When we run **Pub Build** (which compiles our Dart code to JavaScript) and open `test_fuzzy.html` in a browser, it does exactly what we expect:

In the end, it's not that bad even with these limitations and it's already usable.

 There's a new `https://github.com/dart-lang/js-interop` package for Dart-JS interoperation in development right now, which should solve the current limitations of `dart:js`.

Using JavaScript in Dart

In practice, you'll probably need to use a lot of existing code already written in JavaScript from Dart. In this app, we might want to use jQuery's `fadeIn()` and `fadeOut()` functions to show/hide autocomplete.

There're two key methods, `JsFunction.apply()` and `JsObject.callMethod()`, that we'll use and that have the same purpose as in vanilla JavaScript.

We'll add the jQuery package to the project's dependencies in `pubspec.yaml` (Dart packages don't need to contain any Dart code). This package contains only the `jquery.js` file that we add to `index.html`:

```
<script src="packages/jquery/jquery.js"></script>
```

Now, in `DocSearch` class, add a new `JsFunction` `_jQuery` property and initialize it with a proxy object for jQuery in the constructor:

```
_jQuery = context['jQuery'];
```

Finally, update methods to show/hide autocomplete:

```
void showAutocomplete() {
  (_jQuery.apply([_ul]) as JsObject).callMethod('fadeIn', [500]);
}

void hideAutocomplete() {
  (_jQuery.apply([_ul]) as JsObject).callMethod('fadeOut');
}
```

We're basically calling `$(ulElement).fadeIn(500)` and `$(ulElement).fadeOut()`. The `as` keyword means type casting. We're using it here because we know that calling jQuery selector returns a jQuery object and this object has a `fadeIn()`/`fadeOut()` JavaScript method.

Note that the parameters that we used don't need any proxy classes. In situations where we need to pass JavaScript objects as arguments, we have to wrap them with `JsObject.jsify()`, which accepts any Dart collection.

In *Chapter 3*, *The Power of HTML5 with Dart* and *Chapter 4*, *Developing a Mobile App with Dart*, we'll use `dart:js` again with a more complicated examples.

Dart MythBusters

There are some prejudgments about Dart, usually from frontend developers who have never used it or for some reason decided that they don't want to use it at any cost:

- **It's just another abstraction layer like CoffeeScript or TypeScript and will become redundant with ECMAScript 6**: Dart is more than this. It's a full-stack, modern, object-oriented, class-based language with its own standalone VM, IDE, debugger, profiler, and everything (see *Chapter 1*, *Getting Started with Dart*). It takes the best from many of today's languages. You can watch the keynote from Dart Summit 2015 about future plans with Dart (https://www.youtube.com/watch?v=FiXiI2Atexc).

- **It looks like C or Java; it's unnecessarily complicated to do anything with it**: More or less, your code is going to be the same length as vanilla JavaScript plus jQuery. You can see a list of synonyms of Dart and other languages at https://www.dartlang.org/docs/synonyms/.

- **It's not natively supported anywhere and never will**: The Google Dart team worked on the integration of the Dart VM right into the Chrome browser. On March 25, 2015, they announced that they're canceling this effort and instead, they'll work on better integration of Dart and JavaScript while improving the `dart2js` compiler.

  This brought some letdowns from fellow Dartisans, but from a practical point of view, it's probably for the best because even with native Dart support, you would still have to compile your code to JavaScript for other browsers.

  The major problem with Dart is that it's hard to use with existing JavaScript libraries and in real-world applications you'll probably choose between using only Dart or not using Dart at all. This was also one of the reasons why the Angular team didn't choose Dart as their language of choice for Angular 2.0. There's also an experimental compiler in development that is designed to generate readable JavaScript code (https://github.com/dart-lang/dev_compiler).

- **You have to rely on the dart2js compiler**: The `dart2js` compiler is an essential part of the Dart SDK. Dart would never have become popular among developers if the compiler didn't work reliably. For this reason, it's very unlikely that the Dart SDK would come with broken `dart2js`. However, it's true that if your project uses third-party packages, such as AngularDart, which uses custom transformers, it might produce broken code.

- **It's slow and the compiled code is even slower**: In fact, it's the opposite for Dart on Dart VM and `dart2js` is doing pretty good as well. Dart is continuously benchmarked and you can see the results at https://www.dartlang.org/performance/. However, it's questionable whether these tests represent typical use cases for web apps.

- **The compiled JavaScript code is too large**: In *Chapter 1, Getting Started with Dart*, we saw that the difference between the compressed code of compiled Dart and vanilla JavaScript plus jQuery, is very small (we had 37 KB versus 30 KB).

- **You can't use any existing JavaScript**: In this chapter, we've already seen that we can and it's quite simple.

- **Nobody uses it in production**: There are actually quiet a few of them: https://www.dartlang.org/community/who-uses-dart.html.

There are obviously situations where using Dart is too complicated, for example, when you're creating a website and all you have to do is a few fade in/out animations, handling click events, or appending some HTML elements. In these situations, it doesn't make sense to use Dart and it's better to stay with JavaScript. The real advantages of Dart come with more structured and complicated apps.

Summary

This chapter focused on a very practical aspect of Dart. From Streams and the Future-Based API to Ajax, Dart 1.9 took a significant step forward in simplifying the usage of asynchronous APIs using new `async` and `await` keywords. If you don't find yourself familiar with the Future-Based API, at least try to understand the new `async` and `await` features and try to compare Dart's approach to an asynchronous code to what you already know from JavaScript.

We also saw that Dart can work with existing JavaScript code and vice versa. There are some limitations, but the Dart development team announced that they'll focus on simplifying the integration of Dart and JavaScript so the future looks promising.

In the next chapter, we'll focus more on HTML5-specific APIs.

3
The Power of HTML5 with Dart

HTML5 features are already widely supported by most of the modern browsers. In this chapter, we're going to take a look at some of them while building two small apps:

- **Reddit Read Later**: This app fetches the latest posts tagged as `dartlang` from `www.reddit.com` via JSONP, renders them into an HTML list, and allows you to save interesting ones to local IndexedDB
- **Music visualizer**: This app uses the File Drag and Drop API to load music from your computer, analyze frequencies with the Audio API, and draw bar charts on the 2D canvas

On top of that, we'll take a quick look at some technologies commonly used with graphics and games and a few notes about performance, low-level typed arrays, and Dart's Isolates.

If you're planning to support older browsers with limited support of HTML5 features, you can take a look at `http://caniuse.com` to see what's available to you before you start developing.

Both apps are going to heavily use Dart's Future-Based API for all asynchronous operations with `async` and `await` keywords that we talked about in the previous chapter.

Creating the Reddit Read Later app

We can start writing the app right away. We can split it into three separate parts:

- Fetch JSONP data via Reddit API
- Render latest articles into a list
- Let the user save articles into IndexedDB

It's fair to say that this example doesn't use any special HTML5 features apart from IndexedDB. What's interesting here is how it combines multiple things that we've seen in previous chapters, most importantly, the integration of JavaScript within Dart, its Future-Based API, and `JsObject` proxy objects. You can use exactly the same approach for any JavaScript that needs to call Dart callbacks.

Fetching the JSONP data

Simply said, JSONP is a JavaScript object wrapped into a function call and included just like any other JavaScript file (`http://en.wikipedia.org/wiki/JSONP`). Our app is entirely client side. This means that we can't call Ajax requests to servers on a different domain to ours, and unless the remote server returns appropriate **Access-Control-Allow-Origin (ACAO)** headers, all responses will be blocked by the browser due to the same-origin policy (this is mostly for security reasons).

With JSONP, we can avoid browser restrictions and make use of **cross-origin resource sharing**, aka **CORS** (`http://en.wikipedia.org/wiki/Cross-origin_resource_sharing`).

In practice, the JSON response would look like this:

```
{"key1":"value1","key2":"value2"}
```

The JSONP response is wrapped into a function call:

```
callback({'key1': 'value1', 'key2': 'value2'});
```

 Note that included JSONP is just like any other JavaScript file and has full access to the client's browser; therefore, it can be a security threat. Use JSONP only with providers that you trust.

We're going to use JSONP to get a list of the latest posts on `www.reddit.com` that are tagged as `dartlang` from `http://www.reddit.com/r/dartlang/search.json?sort=new&jsonp=callback&limit=10&restrict_sr=on`.

The Reddit API allows us to set a custom callback with the `jsonp` parameter. This is the name of the function that will wrap the entire JavaScript object for us. When using Dart, all JavaScript has to be run in an isolated scope and as we want to be able to refresh Reddit posts anytime we want, we're not going to statically include the preceding URL but rather include it on demand and proxy the JavaScript callback function with ours using `dart:js`:

```dart
// web/main.dart
import 'dart:html';
import 'dart:js';
import 'dart:async';

class RedditReadLater {
  static const String jsonpUrl = 'http://www.reddit.com/...';

  Future<List> refreshReddit() {
    // At this point we have to use [Completer] class to return a
    // Future object and complete it when we process all items
    // in the JavaScript callback.
    var completer = new Completer();

    // Just like window.callback = function() {} in JavaScript.
    // Context is defined in [dart:js] package.
    context['callback'] = (JsObject jsonData) {
      JsArray redditItems = jsonData['data']['children'];
      List<Map<String, String>> items;

      // Iterate all items in the JavaScript array.
      for (int i = 0; i < redditItems.length; i++) {
        JsObject item = redditItems[i]['data'];
        items[i] = ({
          'title': item['title'],
          'url': item['url']
        });
      }
      completer.complete(items);
    };
```

```
        // To dynamically reload data we need to create
        // and append <script> element every time.
        ScriptElement script = new ScriptElement();
        script.src = jsonpUrl;
        document.body.children.add(script);

        // Return a Future object that will be resolved when the
        // included script is loaded and the callback() method called.
        return completer.future;
    }

  void renderReddit(UListElement targetUl, List items) {
        // Remove all children and populate it with new ones.
        var frag = new DocumentFragment();
        for (Map<String, String>item in items) {
          /* Fill the <ul> list with items */
        }
    }
}
```

 For a detailed explanation of the Reddit API, refer to
http://www.reddit.com/dev/api.

Now we can write the stub code for our main() function that will use the Future
object from refreshReddit():

```
void main() {
  var readLater = new RedditReadLater();

  // We can set an optional parameter "_" which is required by
  // onClick stream listener although we don't need it.
  refresh([_]) async {
    var items = await readLater.refreshReddit();
    readLater.renderReddit(
        document.querySelector('#reddit-list'), items);
  }
```

```
document.querySelector('#refresh-btn').onClick.listen(refresh);

    refresh();
}
```

Our HTML template for this app is going to be very short:

```
<body>
    <h2>Latest posts on reddit.com/r/dartlang
      [<a href="#" id="refresh-btn">refresh</a>]
    </h2>
    <ul id="reddit-list"></ul>

    <h2>Read later</h2>
    <ul id="saved-articles"></ul>
</body>
```

The final app filled with posts from `www.reddit.com` will look like this in the browser:

When we know how to fetch and display data via the Reddit API, we can save them to IndexedDB.

IndexedDB

IndexedDB is a transactional client-side storage API with support for high performance searches using indices and is implemented in almost every browser (including mobile browsers). It's designed specifically to store JavaScript objects.

 For more information, you can refer to `http://www.w3.org/TR/IndexedDB/` or `https://developer.mozilla.org/en-US/docs/Web/API/IndexedDB_API`.

There are also some restrictions for IndexedDB:

- The database size is usually limited to tens of MB, although this limitation varies over different browsers. If you want to store a large amount of data, make sure your targeted platform can handle it.

- Your application can use multiple databases, although the size limit in browsers might be per database and also per domain.

- The same-origin policy applies to IndexedDB as with any other resource in JavaScript.

It's a good practice to check whether a client's browser supports HTML5 APIs that might not be available in older browsers. With the `dart:indexed_db` Dart package, you can check it thanks to `IdbFactory.supported`:

```
import 'dart:indexed_db' as idb;
if (!idb.IdbFactory.supported) {
    return;
}
```

During development, it's very useful when you can see what's in your IndexedDB right in Dartium's Developer Tools:

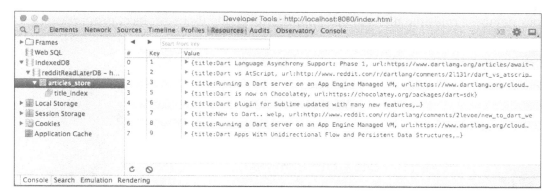

Suppose you end up in a situation where your object store is corrupted or you want to test the behavior when the database doesn't exist yet. In this case, you can right-click on the object store name in Developer Tools and select the **Clear** option from the context menu, and remove it completely.

Initializing IndexedDB

First, include the `dart:indexed_db` package with a prefix because it contains class names that are already used in `dart:html` (for example, the `Request` class):

```
import 'dart:indexed_db' as idb;
```

To create or open a database, call:

```
var db = await window.indexedDB.open('databaseName', version: 1,
    onUpgradeNeeded: onUpgradeNeededCallback
);
```

The `onUpgradeNeededCallback` function is called when you're opening a database with this name for the first time or when the version number is higher than the version of the currently existing database that allows you to migrate to a newer database structure.

Records in the database are stored in **object stores**, which is much like a database table from relational databases. Each database can contain multiple object stores independently on each other. As we'll use the object store name and a reference to our database multiple times in our app, we can create them as object properties:

```
static const String objectStoreName = 'articles_store';
idb.Database _db;
```

Creating an object store for our database is very simple:

```
void onUpgradeNeededCallback(idb.VersionChangeEvent e) {
    idb.Database db = (e.target as idb.Request).result;
    var store = db.createObjectStore(
        objectStoreName, autoIncrement: true);
}
```

A callback to onUpgradeNeeded is the only place where you can create new object stores. Setting autoIncrement to true makes an object store to take care of generating unique keys for new records inserted to the object store.

Fetching stored records

All operations in IndexedDB are performed via transactions. The first argument to transaction() is its scope, which can be multiple object stores. The second argument is a mode that can be readonly or readwrite. You can perform multiple readonly operations concurrently but only one readwrite operation at the time.

We're going to simply get a cursor object that points at the beginning of our object store and gets one record at a time. When used as a stream, it fires events for every record in the object store. The autoAdvance parameter set to true makes the cursor automatically move to the next record; otherwise, we would have to call the next() method manually:

```
loadDataFromDB() async {
    var trans = _db.transaction(objectStoreName, 'readonly');
    var store = trans.objectStore(objectStoreName);

    Map<String, Map<String, String>>dbItems = new Map();
    var cursors = store.openCursor(
        autoAdvance: true).asBroadcastStream();
```

```
    // Bind an event which is called for each record.
    cursors.listen((cursor) {
      dbItems[cursor.key] = cursor.value;
    });

    // Wait until all records have emitted their events.
    await cursors.length;
    renderReadLaterItems(dbItems);
}
```

The `renderReadLaterItems()` method just renders all records into a list just like the `renderReddit()` method.

You can, of course, fetch a single record by its `key`, which, again, returns a `Future` object:

```
store.getObject(key)
```

Saving records

We need to update the `renderReddit()` method to handle our `onClick` event, add a clicked item to the object store, and reload all records:

```
void renderReddit(UListElement targetUl, List items) {
  var frag = new DocumentFragment();
  for (Map<String, String>item in items) {
    AnchorElement aElm = new AnchorElement()
      ..text = '[save]';
      ..href = '#';
      ..onClick.listen((e) async {
        e.preventDefault();
        await this._save(item);
        // Let's not worry about performance now.
        loadDataFromDB();
      });

    /* … */
    frag.append(liElm);
  }
  targetUl.children.clear();
  targetUl.append(frag);
}
```

Here we're meeting `Future` objects again:

```
Future _save(Map item) {
  var trans = this._db.transaction(objectStoreName, 'readwrite');
  var store = trans.objectStore(objectStoreName);

  // add() method persists record and returns a [Future] object.
  // Item's key is generated by our object store.
  store.add(item).then((addedKey) => print(addedKey));
  // We're not using await because only the transactions can tell
  // when it's finished. [Future.then()] is just better here.
 // [Transaction.completed] is an instance of [Future].
  return trans.completed;
}
```

Deleting records

Note that in order to remove a record from the object store, we need to know its database key:

```
Future _delete(key) {
  var trans = this._db.transaction(objectStoreName, 'readwrite');
  // Delete record by its generated key.
  trans.objectStore(objectStoreName).delete(key);
  return trans.completed;
}
```

Similarly, we can remove all records:

```
trans.objectStore(objectStoreName).clear();
```

Indices

Although we didn't need any indicies in our app, it's worth mentioning how to use them. Just like all operations that modify database structures, we have to define indices in the `onUpgradeNeeded` callback:

```
store.createIndex('index_name', 'col_to_index', unique: true);
```

If we wanted, for example, to search our saved Reddit posts by their title, we would set the index like this:

```
store.createIndex('title_index', 'title');
```

Let's set a search query to filter, say, only those posts that start with the letter R:

```
var trans = this._db.transaction(objectStoreName, 'readonly');
var store = trans.objectStore(objectStoreName);
var index = store.index(titleIndex);

var range = new idb.KeyRange.lowerBound('R');
var cursors = index.openCursor(
    range: range, autoAdvance: true).asBroadcastStream();
cursors.listen((cursor) {
  print(cursor.value['title']);
});
```

This is very similar to fetching all records, as we did a moment ago.

Note that we're opening the cursor over `index` instead of the entire store and passing a `range` argument, which is basically our search query. The `idb.KeyRange` item has four named constructors that you can use:

Key name	Description
KeyRange.bound(lower, upper)	Matches all values between these two bounds.
KeyRange.lowerBound(bound)	Matches all values with this lower bound and everything after it.
KeyRange.only(value)	Single value key range. Indexed column needs to match this value.
KeyRange.upperBound(bound)	Matches all values with this upper bound and everything before.

 Bounds don't need to be numbers. You can use strings for bounds as well.

Compared to any SQL-like database, indices in IndexedDB are very primitive, but thanks to its simplicity, IndexedDB can be available even on mobile devices with very limited resources.

Polishing the application

The finalized application can look like the following screenshot. You probably don't want to rewrite all the source code by yourself, so feel free to download the source code for this chapter and see how it's done.

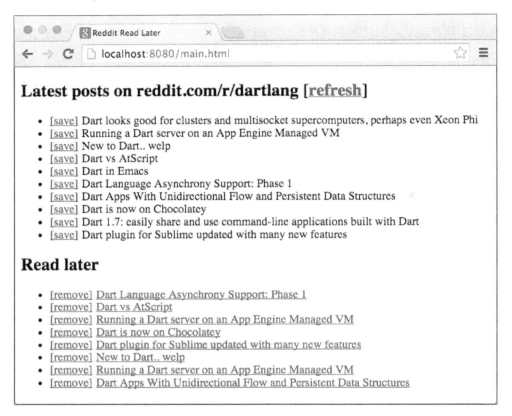

LocalStorage versus IndexedDB

LocalStorage is a key-value storage that can be used instead of IndexedDB in some situations. For example, in the application that we have just created, we could use LocalStorage instead of IndexedDB without any problem, but remember that LocalStorage is a very primitive storage and in terms of use cases, it's like cookies with less restrictions.

If you're looking for a universal storage engine with multiple backends integrated, take a look at `https://pub.dartlang.org/packages/lawndart`.

What about WebSQL?

WebSQL was supposed to be a SQL variant that could run in clients' browsers. However, it's been discontinued by W3C and probably won't be supported by any browser in the future because the only available implementation was SQLite.

It's recommended that you use IndexedDB instead.

 You should remember that IndexedDB isn't an SQL-like database. It's not even a drop in replacement for WebSQL.

Music visualizer

Our second app will be a simple music visualizer using the Audio API, File Drag and Drop API, and Canvas. We'll split it into two parts: first, the drop area for a music file, which will load its content using `readAsDataUrl()`, and place its content into the `src` attribute of the audio element. Then, we connect various filters to the audio stream and read its raw output from the audio analyzer.

 Dartium doesn't support some common audio/video formats, such as *.mp3 (`http://www.chromium.org/audio-video`). Although you can enable it manually, try using *.mp4, *.webm, or *.m4a instead.

We can start with a short HTML snippet:

```
<!-- web/index.html -->
<body>
  <h1>Chapter 03 music visualizer</h1>

  <audio autoplay loop controls="true">
    Your browser does not support the audio element.
  </audio>

  <div id="fileDrop">drop music file here</div>
  <canvas width="300" height="50" id="canvas"></canvas>
</body>
```

Now, add the Drag and Drop event listeners to the `#fileDrop` element:

```dart
// web/main.dart
import 'dart:html';
import 'dart:math';

class MusicVisualizer {
  AudioElement _audio;

  MusicVisualizer() {
    Element dropZone = document.querySelector('#fileDrop');
    _audio = document.querySelector('audio');

    // This is the event that we need.
    dropZone.onDrop.listen((MouseEvent event) {
      event.preventDefault();
      event.stopPropagation();
      // Although, user can drop multiple files we're interested
      // only in the first one.
      File file = event.dataTransfer.files.first;
      var reader = new FileReader();

      document.querySelector('h1').text = file.name;

      // When the file is loaded we want to add our filters.
      reader.onLoad.listen(audioLoaded);
      reader.readAsDataUrl(file);
    });

    // Prevent default browser behavior because by default
    // browser would open the file and we wouldn't be
    // able to read its content.
    dropZone.onDragOver.listen((MouseEvent event) {
      event.preventDefault();
      event.stopPropagation();
    });
  }

  void audioLoaded(ProgressEvent event) { }
}

void main() {
  var music = new MusicVisualizer();
}
```

In total, there are seven events related to Drag and Drop: onDragStart, onDragEnd, onDrag, onDragEnter, onDragLeave, onDragOver, and onDrop.

We only care about onDrop and onDragOver, so we can leave the rest unused.

Now, we're going to add three filters (in the context of the Audio API, they call it audio nodes). Two frequency filters, lowpass and highpass, can cut off frequencies lower or higher than the specified threshold. We'll use them to cut off frequencies that aren't audible to the human ear because it doesn't make sense to visualize sounds that we can't hear. The last filter is the audio analyzer, which we can use to access raw audio data.

We'll chain all three filters from the audio source to the destination where the destination is the default audio output.

```
source => filter1 => filter2 => analyzer => destination
```

In other words, we're going to add three nodes between the source and the destination and hook up the analyzer node to access raw audio data.

 There are other types of filters in addition to these three (https://developer.mozilla.org/en-US/docs/Web/API/BiquadFilterNode.type). We're not including all of them here because their usage is very similar.

Actually, if we just want to visualize the audio stream, we don't even need to use filters but we're including them here to make the example a little more complex:

```dart
// web/main.dart
import 'dart:web_audio';
import 'dart:typed_data';
/* … */

class MusicVisualizer {
  AnalyserNode _analyser;
  /* … */

  void audioLoaded(ProgressEvent event) {
    // Access audio file as Base64 encoded string.
    _audio.src = (event.target as FileReader).result;

    AudioContext audioCtx = new AudioContext();
    MediaElementAudioSourceNode source =
```

```
        audioCtx.createMediaElementSource(_audio);

      // Object that we'll use to access raw audio data.
      _analyser = audioCtx.createAnalyser();

      BiquadFilterNode filter1 = audioCtx.createBiquadFilter();
      filter1.type = 'lowpass';
      // Cut off all frequencies above this threshold.
      filter1.frequency.value = 20000;

      BiquadFilterNode filter2 = audioCtx.createBiquadFilter();
      filter2.type = 'highpass';
      // Cut off all frequencies below this threshold.
      filter2.frequency.value = 80;

      // The actual filter chaining.
      source.connectNode(filter1);
      filter1.connectNode(filter2);
      filter2.connectNode(_analyser);
      _analyser.connectNode(audioCtx.destination);

      // Play the audio file when it's loaded.
      _audio.play();

      this.run();
    }

    void run() { /* We'll write it in a moment */ }
  }
```

Note that we're also including two more packages:

- The `dart:web_audio` package has classes that work with the Audio API.

- The `dart:typed_data` package has low-level, type-specific structures. You usually don't need to work with such data structures unless you need really high performance code or when you're working with raw data, as with the Audio API or with WebGL and matrices.

Now we can group frequencies in the audio into N groups and draw them in a loop.

For timing, we could just use `setTimeout()` but with HTML5, we have a better method called `requestAnimationFrame()`. This delays the function call until the browser thinks it's the time to redraw the screen (usually trying to keep stable 60 fps):

```
int _bars = 300;

void run() {
  _canvas = document.querySelector('#canvas');
  _ctx = _canvas.getContext('2d');

  window.requestAnimationFrame(draw);
}

void draw(double time) {
  // Create and instance of [Uint8List] with fixed length.
  var arr = new Uint8List(_analyser.frequencyBinCount);
  // Flush current audio data into the array.
  _analyser.getByteFrequencyData(arr);

  // Divide all frequencies into _bars groups and sum them.
  List<int> barChart = new List.filled(_bars, 0);
  for (int i = 0; i < arr.length; i++) {
    int index = (i / (arr.length / _bars)).floor();
    barChart[index] += arr[i];
  }

  // max/min method are defined in [dart:math]
  double chartMax = barChart.reduce(max).toDouble();
  double chartMin = barChart.reduce(min).toDouble();

  // Clear canvas; this is a small hack that clears canvas
  // faster than calling [fillRect()] or [clearRect()].
  _canvas.width = _canvas.width;
  int barWidth = (_canvas.width / _bars).round();

  // Draw green rectangle for each bar.
  _ctx.fillStyle = "#00ff00";

  for (int i = 0; i < _bars; i++) {
    // Height of a bar is relative to the size of the highest bar.
    double height = _canvas.height *
        ((barChart[i] - chartMin) / chartMax);
    // Coordinates 0x0 are at the top left corner.
    // [fillRect()] takes top left and bottom right corner of the
```

```
        // rectangle you want to draw and fills it with color
        // set with [fillStyle].
        _ctx.fillRect(barWidth * i, _canvas.height - height,
            barWidth * (i + 1), _canvas.height);
    }

    // Draw again when the browser is ready.
    window.requestAnimationFrame(draw);
}
```

Instead of drawing bars with rectangles, we could also use lineStyle, lineWidth, moveTo(), lineTo(), and stroke(). At the end, it would probably be more complicated because with moveTo() and lineTo(), you are setting the center of the line that you're going to draw. With 1 px line width, this means a 0.5 px overlap on each side, which would create blurred lines (unless, you add 0.5 px to each coordinate in moveTo() and lineTo()).

If you look at the code, you will notice that there are quite a lot of operations. Depending on the music file that you drop to #dropZone, getByteFrequencyData() fills arr with, for example, 1,024 items that you iterate right after that and then calls fillRect() 300 times. This all is processed in 60 fps.

The final app could look like this with a little CSS:

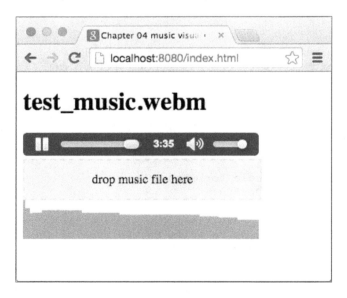

Other noteworthy APIs and libraries

The goal of this book is not to go through all the APIs that come with HTML5, but there are some that are worth taking a look at, including some interesting Dart libraries. You probably won't use them on a daily basis, but it's good to know that there's such things available to you.

Typed lists for fast numeric computing

Even though everything in Dart is an object and the VM is very well optimized, there's a built-in `dart:typed_data` library, which we already mentioned in the audio visualizer app. This library contains data structures (mostly lists) with fixed size n-bit signed / unsigned integers / floats. In other words, lists that can contain only n-bit numbers and no objects.

In practice, if we knew we wanted to store only 8-bit values (that's 0-255) in an array, we could use the `Uint8List` class instead of `List<int>`. This could represent, for example, image colors:

```dart
import 'dart:io';
import 'dart:typed_data';

main() {
  const max = 10 * 1000 * 1000; // 10 million elements
  print("My PID: $pid");

  var objectList = new Uint8List(max);
  // Fill with values.
  for (int i = 0; i < max; i++) objectList[i] = i % 255;

  // Sum values.
  int total = 0;
  for (int i = 0; i < max; i++) total += objectList[i];
  print(total);

  // Pause here so we can check memory usage.
  stdin.readLineSync();
}
```

Its usage is exactly the same as a normal `List` object. This version with the `Uint8List` typed list takes 21.1 MB of memory while the version with `List<int>` takes 49.1 MB of memory on a 32-bit standalone Dart VM.

For more in-depth information, read `https://www.dartlang.org/articles/numeric-computation/`.

vector_math

The third-party `vector_math` package is a collection of 2D, 3D, and 4D vector and matrix types and collision detection algorithms. You're probably not going to use `vector_math` on daily basis, but it's definitely good to know that there is such a package if you were looking for high performance (in terms of browser capability) computing. Games and 3D graphic applications are the most common usages.

SIMD

Single instruction, multiple data (SIMD) is a set of instructions that can perform a single operation on multiple data simultaneously. When SIMD instructions are used properly, it usually means significant performance improvement.

Since August 2013, SIMD is available to you in Dart via `Int32x4` and `Float32x4` classes (`https://www.dartlang.org/articles/simd/`).

The current version of `vector_math` already uses SIMD instructions; therefore, you don't need to worry about implementing vector and matrix manipulations by yourself and you can leave all the difficult work to `vector_math`, which is already well optimized.

Of course, SIMD is available only in Dartium right now. The future looks promising for all non-Dart browsers too. Intel, in collaboration with Google and Mozilla, already runs SIMD code in JavaScript and is trying to bring the JavaScript SIMD API into the ES7 version of the JavaScript standard (`https://01.org/blogs/tlcounts/2014/bringing-simd-javascript`).

WebGL

WebGL and technologies around it are such a vast topic that they could easily cover the entire book.

The current browser version of WebGL is based on OpenGL ES 2.0, which is used in most of today's mobile devices (iPad, and iPhone 5S, and newer devices also support OpenGL ES 3.0).

The source code for this chapter contains a small demo with a rotating 3D cube and a triangular pyramid. We're not going to look into this example here because vanilla WebGL is crazy complicated, and in practice, you'd probably use a third-party library. By the way, this very basic example has 350 lines of code.

three.dart

Probably the most popular JavaScript 3D engine nowadays is three.js and three.dart is its port in Dart (`https://github.com/threeDart/three.dart`). Three.dart uses `vector_math` heavily.

If you're thinking about developing a game or any visually complicated 3D app, don't start writing it from scratch with pure WebGL, use a 3D engine instead. Even when it looks like writing everything by yourself will suit your needs and result in a better performance, usually it ends up the exact opposite. High-performance code with vector and matrix optimizations with SIMD is complicated and requires a deeper understanding of how CPUs and browsers' VMs work inside.

StageXL

Until HTML5 became relatively common, the only way to create rich web apps was to use Adobe Flash. Switching from Flash to JavaScript or Dart is very time-consuming because you have to rewrite absolutely everything from scratch. StageXL uses mostly the same API as Flash and is designed for easy migration from Adobe Flash to HTML5 and Dart (`http://www.stagexl.org`).

Box2D and play_phaser

Box2D (`https://github.com/google/box2d.dart`) is a 2D physics library that is a port of Java JBox2D, which is a port of C++ Box2D. It's been developed since January 2012 by Dominic Hamon, a former employee of Electronic Arts, LucasArts, and Google. It uses most of the features of `vector_math` that are currently available.

The play_phaser library (`https://github.com/playif/play_phaser`) is a full-featured 2D game engine with a WebGL renderer, physics, an audio mixer, animation engine, and so on—basically, all you might need.

Isolates and Web Workers

Dart supports multithreaded programming using the Isolate API. Isolates are execution contexts that can only access variables from the same isolate.

Isolates are similar to threads in that they can run on multiple CPUs (and cores), but unlike threads, isolates don't share the same memory, and therefore, all communication between them must be done by sending messages.

The Isolate API runs in both standalone Dart VMs and browsers where the browser implementation is based internally on Web Workers (therefore, there's no Web Worker class in Dart). We'll come back to isolates in *Chapter 9, Writing Native Extensions for the Standalone Dart VM*.

Summary

In this chapter, we took a look at some HTML5-specific APIs.

We used IndexedDB to store, fetch, and delete records. Remember that WebSQL has been discontinued due to the lack of independent implementations, and you shouldn't use it any more. The Drag and Drop API is available in Dart via the `onDrag*` event listeners on HTML elements.

The Audio API has access to raw audio data through low-level data structures and can modify it using various filters. For animations with a stable frame rate, it's recommended that you use `requestAnimationFrame()`. Canvases with 2D and WebGL contexts can be fully experienced in Dart.

We also used the `dart:js` library to create a Dart callback function, which is later called by JavaScript and that converts JavaScript proxy objects into Dart objects.

In the next chapter, we're going to look at developing applications for mobile devices using Dart. Also, we'll take a look at some more HTML5 APIs that are specific to mobile devices and CSS3 3D transformations that run on both desktop and mobile.

4
Developing a Mobile App with Dart

In this chapter, we're going to take a quick look at CSS3 3D transformations and introduce some more HTML5 APIs that are specific to mobile devices. With the knowledge gained from the previous chapters, we'll develop four small apps that will make use of the things that we've already learned:

- **Basics of CSS3 transformations**: We'll learn basics about axes, movement, and rotation in the 3D space and how can we use them to transform HTML elements using CSS3.

- **3D bookshelf rotated using HTML5 DeviceOrientation events**: After we learn how to perform basic operations in 3D with CSS3, we can make a slightly more complicated app with nested 3D objects and textures. In order to make it more interactive, we'll listen to DeviceOrientation events and rotate the entire scene in 3D as you rotate your device.

- **Track position and distance using HTML5's GeoLocation API with the Google Maps API**: We'll see how to use the Google Maps JavaScript API to track and draw your movement while calculating total distance and drawing the track to the map. For the entire communication between Dart and JavaScript, we'll use the dart:js library.

- **Draw into the 2D canvas using onTouch events**: We already know how to draw into canvas from the previous chapter; this time, we'll see how to combine it with touch events.

Although some of the APIs covered in this chapter are mobile-specific, you can emulate them in Chrome or Dartium.

300 ms tap delay

By default, mobile browsers add artificial 300 ms delay between the time you release your finger (`onTouchEnd`) and before a click event is triggered. This is a nice accessibility feature for normal web pages that aren't optimized for mobile browsers, but for web apps that are designed to look and feel native, this is unwanted behavior.

There used to be some nasty workarounds, but browser vendors decided to remove this delay for mobile-friendly (or mobile-optimized) websites. This means that pages that use this header aren't affected by tap delay:

```
<meta name="viewport" content="width=device-width">
```

This `meta` variable tells the browser to set its width to the device width with respect to the pixel density. For example, for iPhone 6 with 1334 x 750 screen resolution, and pixel density 2, the page will be rendered in a browser window with a 667 x 375 resolution. Now as a side effect, it also turns off the tap delay.

We recommend that you use this header for all examples in this chapter unless you know for sure that you don't want it.

Basics of CSS3 transformations

All modern browsers already support CSS transforms, including mobile browsers. For the first two apps, we'll use four new statements from CSS3 heavily:

- `transform`: Move, rotate, scale, or skew the HTML element using `translate[X,Y,Z](v)`, `rotate[X,Y,Z](v)`, `scale[X,Y,Z](v)`, and `skew[X,Y](v)`, respectively. All these basic transformations have their 3D alternative, such as `rotate3d(x, y, z, angle)`, that you can use to set transformations in all three dimensions with one statement.

  If you want to perform more transformations on an element, you have to set all of them in a single CSS statement, for example, `transform: rotateY(90deg) translateX(100px);`.

- `transform-style`: Using `flat` or `preserve-3d` options, you can tell the browser whether you want to apply 3D transformations from parent elements to their child. By default, the browser takes all transformations on a per-element basis, which means that if you, for example, rotate the parent element and then rotate its child elements, the browser will perform rotations independently.

- `perspective`: Set the perspective depth for this element and all its children as a distance from the element to the viewer. Changing this value doesn't change the size of elements, as we'll see in the second app.

- `transform-origin`: This statement is mostly useful for rotation. It lets you set a point around which rotation will be performed. By default, the origin is set to the element's center.

 All these CSS3 statements are currently available on mobile browsers only with the prefix `-webkit-`.

Axes

The coordinate system for transformations is very obvious: the *x* and *y* axes are like those you're probably used to. The *z* axis goes in the direction to/from you. The center of coordinates for each element is in its center by default.

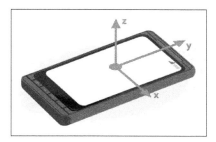

Source: `https://developer.mozilla.org/en-US/docs/Web/Guide/Events/Orientation_and_motion_data_explained`

Hello world in 3D

It's time to see CSS3 transformations in action. We're going to rotate this HTML snippet:

```
<body>
  <div id="container">
    <div id="first">Hello</div>
    <div id="second">World!</div>
  </div>
</body>
```

Apply CSS3 with a few 3D transformations:

```
/* Center of perspective for this div will be in [250,50]. */
#container { height: 100px; width: 500px;
            perspective: 300px; position: relative; }
#container div { position: absolute; width: 150px; }
#first { transform: rotateY(30deg) translateX(-85px); }
#second { transform: rotateY(-40deg) translateX(85px); }
```

We're omitting some nonimportant CSS such as font size or colors here in order to make the examples more readable.

In the browser, we'll see rotated div elements with text like this. Note that the white text is just like any other text on the page. Also, transformed elements are just normal div elements that can be adjusted with CSS to what you desire.

This is an important distinction from WebGL, where everything is drawn right into the canvas using shaders and has absolutely nothing to do with HTML.

Both div elements, #first and #second, are positioned absolutely. If we didn't translate their position, they would overlay each other, but at the same time, we can't use just inline-block because the rotated div element takes the same space as when it wasn't rotated. Therefore, it would be even harder to make them look like they're joined together.

Nesting 3D transformed elements

Let's add one more div element to the #first element:

```
<div id="container">
  <div id="first"><div id="third">Nested</div>Hello</div>
  <div id="second">World!</div>
</div>
```

Then, add styles that transform this `div` element as well:

```
#third { transform-origin: 0 0;
         transform: rotateY(110deg); }
```

We want to rotate it around the *y* axis by 110 degrees, centered to the left edge of its parent (that's the effect of the `transform-origin`). This should make the mirrored image of the element look like it's joined to the left edge of `#first` while going slightly to the left and fading away from us. The `#third` element is aligned to the top-left corner of its parent because it's positioned absolutely.

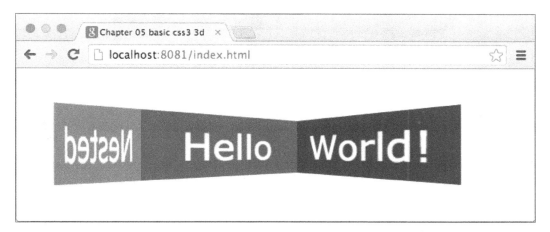

But wait; that's not what we wanted. We can see the back of the `#third` element, which makes the output look like it's mirrored. That's fine but it seems like it's following the same transformation as `#first`.

The reason for this behavior is that the browser flattens transformations for child elements. To avoid this, we'll use `transform-style: preserve-3d`, which we mentioned earlier. Note that `preserve-3d` applies the parent's transformations only to direct children elements. If children elements have other children elements, then they have to use `preserve-3d` as well.

So, we can fix this by adding `transform-style: preserve-3d` to `#first`:

```
#first { /* … */ transform-style: preserve-3d; }
```

Now the result looks like we expected:

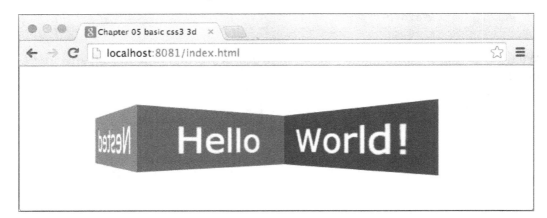

 In some situations, you don't want to see the back of rotated elements. In that case, set `backface-visibility: hidden;`.

If you're confused with all these rotations and translations, don't worry. It's hard to imagine rotating objects in 3D, moreover, combining multiple nested objects and rotating each of them relatively.

Your best friend is Developer Tools. Try changing rotations or translations on the fly, change perspective, and see what effect it has. Also, change `transform-origin` on `#third` and see what happens.

We'll later set transformations in Dart for both `-webkit-` prefixed and nonprefixed versions, such as:

```
element.style.setProperty('transform', 'rotateX...');
// Mobile browsers supporting only prefixed versions.
element.style.setProperty('-webkit-transform', 'rotateX...');
```

A 3D bookshelf with DeviceOrientation events

We already saw the basics, and we can start with a more attractive app, for example:

Each book is made out of six div elements and the shelf itself are five div elements (we don't need the back face):

```
<div id="book-container">
  <div class="book dune-new">
    <div class="front"></div>
    <div class="left"></div>
    <div class="right"></div>
    <div class="back"></div>
    <div class="top"></div>
    <div class="bottom"></div>
  </div>

  <div class="book dune-old"><!-- 6 book's faces again --></div>
  <div class="shelf"><!-- 5 shelf's faces --></div>
</div>
```

The CSS for this example is not that complicated; there are just a lot of transformations. Feel free to open this example in the browser and check where each `div` element is positioned:

```
/* Entire document is using single perspective. */
body { perspective: 500px; }

#book-container { transform-style: preserve-3d; text-align:center;
   /* Try manually rotating the scene. */
   /* transform: rotateX(-40deg) rotateY(20deg); */
}

.book { display: inline-block; width: 150px; height: 230px;
        transform-style: preserve-3d; position: relative; }
.book > div { position: absolute; }
.book > .front { transform: translateZ(15px); }
.book > .left { width: 30px; transform-origin: 0 0;
                transform: rotateY(-90deg) translateX(-15px); }
.book > .top { height: 30px; width: 145px;
                transform: rotateX(90deg) translateZ(10px); }
.book > .back { transform: rotateY(180deg) translateZ(15px); }
.book > .right { height: 220px; width: 30px;
        transform: rotateY(90deg) translateZ(130px) translateY(5px);}
.book > .bottom { height: 30px; width: 145px;
                transform: rotateX(90deg) translateZ(-210px); }
```

For the sake of simplicity, both books are the same size: 150 px width, 230 px height, and 30 px deep. Let's take a look at some interesting parts:

- `.book`: This wraps all the faces for each book. When we want to position each book on the page, we don't want to move each face separately. Rather, move/rotate the entire container, and all the faces inside will transform relatively to it because of `preserve-3d`. Note that we're setting `display: inline-block` and hardcoding the width and height to be sure how much space each book is going to take no matter what the faces inside do.

- `.book > div`: All faces are positioned absolutely, which means that they will be aligned to the top-left corner of their parent `.book` element.

- `.book > .front`: This moves the front face 15 px (that's half of the book's depth) along the z axis, because we want to keep the center of the book in its center for all axes. This face has the book's cover image set as its `background-image`.

- .book > .left: This (highlighted in blue) moves the transform origin to the top-left corner of the div element, rotates it by 90 degrees, and moves it 15 px back along the z axis. That's all we need to do for this face because on the x and y axis, it's already where we want it to be thanks to transform-origin: 0 0;.

- .book > .top: This is very similar to .left. We just want to move it a little bit down to make the book look like it's a hardcover. Note that when rotating div elements, you also rotate axes, and that's why we're translating along z and not y.

- #book-container: This wraps the entire bookshelf with books. We want to rotate the entire scene and not just the books; we'll apply transformations to this wrapper using Dart.

Creating a shelf with a wood texture works on exactly the same principle, so we don't need to do it here again.

Now, in Dart, we'll listen to the deviceorientation event of the window object, which fires every time the device rotates. In reality, this event will be fired many times per second because the sensors aren't precise and will probably fire events even when your mobile device is lying on the table:

```
window.addEventListener('deviceorientation',
    (DeviceOrientationEvent e) {
  print(e.alpha);
  print(e.beta);
  print(e.gamma);
});
```

These are the three angles that we can use to set the rotation on our #book-container element:

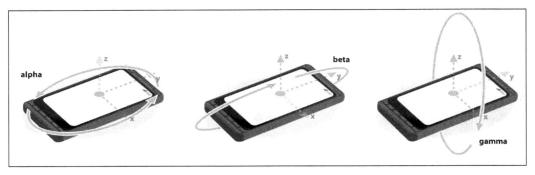

Source: https://developer.mozilla.org/en-US/docs/Web/Guide/Events/Orientation_and_motion_data_explained

 Orientation works differently on mobile devices and computers. As a rule of thumb on computers, the reference point is not the screen but the keyboard instead. Therefore, the axis will be probably shuffled.

This code expects that you're running it on a computer, so you can easily test rotations with Developer Tools:

```
// web/main.dart
import 'dart:html';

void main() {
  HtmlElement container =
      document.querySelector('#book-container');

  int initRotationX = null;
  int initRotationY = null;

  window.addEventListener('deviceorientation',
      (DeviceOrientationEvent e) {
    // These parameters are expected on a computer.
    if (e.beta != null && e.gamma != null) {
      // Make the rotation relative to the initial position,
      // not [0, 0, 0].
      if (initRotationX == null && initRotationY == null) {
        initRotationX = e.beta.round();
```

```
        initRotationY = e.gamma.round();
    }

    int rotY = (e.gamma.round() - initRotationY);
    int rotX = -(e.beta.round() - initRotationX);
    // String value for the CSS statement.
    var transform = "rotateX(${rotX}deg) rotateY(${rotY}deg)";

    container.style.setProperty('transform', transform);
    // Mobile browsers support only prefixed versions.
    container.style.setProperty('-webkit-transform', transform);
    }
  });
}
```

Now we can open Developer Tools and simulate different rotations. In the **Emulation** tab, click on **Sensors** and you should see three input fields, each for one axis.

When you change β (beta) and γ (gamma), the entire scene will rotate.

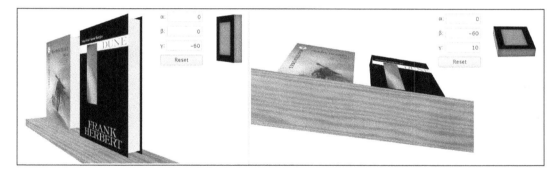

With quite a short Dart code, we created an app that can react to device rotation and can change CSS styles dynamically from Dart.

As we mentioned earlier, it's okay if you find 3D manipulations complicated and confusing. We encourage you to download the source code for this chapter, play around with CSS transformations, and see what happens.

Obviously, making complicated 3D objects is nearly impossible. There are already tools that make the creation of 3D objects from `div` elements easier by generating HTML structure and CSS3 for you. You can take a look at one of them, called Tridiv (`http://tridiv.com`), and note that you can create quite nice stuff with it. But remember, embedding such complicated objects will have significant impact on performance.

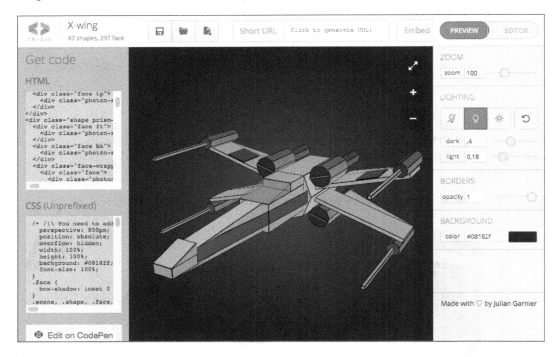

CSS3 transformations, compared to WebGL, are very primitive. There's no built-in lighting renderer, although there's an alternative in JavaScript and CSS3 called Photon (`http://photon.attasi.com/`), which is good for small projects with a few transformed elements, such as the bookshelf example that we created a moment ago. For larger objects such as the X-Wing from Tridiv, it's quite slow. The same object rendered with WebGL would run smoothly without any problem even on slower computers.

 You can read a small comparison of CSS3 transformation and WebGL here: `http://blog.teamtreehouse.com/3d-in-the-browser-webgl-versus-css-3d-transforms`.

In Chrome and Dartium, you can check whether various rendering techniques are hardware accelerated right in your browser at `chrome://gpu/`.

Position and distance tracker with the GeoLocation API and Google Maps API

In *Chapter 2*, *Practical Dart*, we learned about the `dart:js` library. We saw that we can proxy JavaScript objects using the `JsObject` class in Dart. We're going to use the `JsObject` class a lot right now because this app will use the Google Maps API, which is a JavaScript API that we'll control from Dart.

 There's a Dart wrapper (`https://pub.dartlang.org/packages/google_maps`) for the Google Maps API, which you would probably prefer in a real-world app, but for demonstration purposes, we'll write everything by ourselves.

First, include the Google Maps API before including any Dart script:

```
<script src="http://maps.../api/js?libraries=geometry"></script>
<script type="application/dart" src="main.dart"></script>
```

Note the `?libraries=geometry` parameter in the URL. This tells Google to include an additional library in the API, which we need in order to calculate the distance between two GPS locations.

We'll initialize Google Map and assign Dart proxies to JavaScript objects:

```
import 'dart:html';
import 'dart:js';
import 'dart:async';

void main() {
  double totalDistance = 0.0;

  // My last position as a JavaScript LatLng object.
  JsObject lastPos;
  JsObject mapsApi = context['google']['maps'];

  // Reference to an object that we'll instantiate multiple times.
  JsObject jsLatLng = mapsApi['LatLng'];
  // We'll keep listener subscription in a variable
  // because we want to be able to unsubscribe.
  StreamSubscription<Geoposition> locSubscr = null;
  // Proxy object to computeDistanceBetween().
```

```
    JsFunction jsDistance =
        mapsApi['geometry']['spherical']['computeDistanceBetween'];

    HtmlElement distanceElm, distanceFromLastElm;
    HtmlElement statusElm, mapCanvas;
    ButtonElement btnStart, btnStop;

    /* Assign HTML elements to Dart variables. */

    // Convert Dart Map into a JavaScript object.
    JsObject mapOptions = new JsObject.jsify({
      "zoom": 2,
        "center": new JsObject.jsify({ 'lat': 20.0, 'lng': -30.0}),
        "mapTypeId": mapsApi['MapTypeId']['ROADMAP']
    });

    // Init Google Map.
    var map = new JsObject(mapsApi['Map'], [mapCanvas, mapOptions]);

    // Method called after receiving the first coordinates.
    void init(Coordinates c) {
      lastPos = new JsObject(jsLatLng, [c.latitude, c.longitude]);

      // Call two methods on JsObject proxy.
      map.callMethod('setCenter', [lastPos]);
      map.callMethod('setZoom', [16]);

      // Draw a circle to the map that marks my initial position
      // by calling JavaScript object constructor.
      new JsObject(mapsApi['Circle'], [new JsObject.jsify({
        'strokeColor': '#FF0000', 'strokeOpacity': 0.8,
        'strokeWeight': 2, 'fillColor': '#FF0000',
        'fillOpacity': 0.8, 'map': map,
        'center': lastPos, 'radius': 10
      })]);
    }

    /* … */
}
```

Now when we want to know our current position, we can use:

```
window.navigator.geolocation.getCurrentPosition()
```

This code returns a `Future<Geoposition>` object. We can also listen to every change in position by subscribing to the `watchPosition()` stream:

```
window.navigator.geolocation.watchPosition()
```

Unfortunately, `getCurrentPosition()` doesn't work properly in every browser, so we have to be able to handle everything in `watchPosition()` alone.

 Currently, there's a bug in Dartium that causes the GeoLocation API to throw an error when used, so in Dart SDK 1.9, the only way to run this example is to compile it to JavaScript with `dart2js`.

We also add two buttons, start and stop, that bind and unbind listeners, respectively:

```dart
void main() {

  /* ... */

  void updateStatus() {
    statusElm.text = (locSubscr == null ? 'Stopped' : 'Running');
  }
  updateStatus();

  // Bind event listeners.
  void bindListeners() {
    // Get current location.
    window.navigator.geolocation.getCurrentPosition().then((p) {
      print(p.coords.latitude);
      print(p.coords.longitude);

      init(p.coords);
    }, onError: (PositionError e) => print(e.toString()));

    // Listen to every change in position.
    // We want to keep reference to the subscription to be
    // able to cancel the subscription later.
    locSubscr = window.navigator.geolocation
        .watchPosition().listen((Geoposition pos) {
      if (lastPos == null) init(pos.coords);

      // Create an instance of LatLng JavaScript object.
      var currPos = new JsObject(
          jsLatLng, [pos.coords.latitude, pos.coords.longitude]);
```

```dart
    // Center map to my current location.
    map.callMethod('setCenter', [currPos]);

    var path = [lastPos, currPos];

    // Create a line and draw it to the map.
    var lineOptions = new JsObject.jsify({
      'strokeColor': '#0000FF',
      'strokeOpacity': 1.0,
      'strokeWeight': 3,
      'map': map
    });
    var line = new JsObject(mapsApi['Polyline'], [lineOptions]);
    line.callMethod('setPath', [new JsObject.jsify(path)]);

    // Convert the returned variable to double.
    // jsDistance is our [jsFunction] proxy.
    var dist = double.parse(jsDistance.apply(path).toString());
    distanceFromLastElm.text = dist.toString();

    totalDistance += dist;
    // Keep this position for the next event fired.
    lastPos = currPos;

    distanceElm.text = totalDistance.toString();
  });
}

void cancelListeners(e) {
  locSubscr.cancel();
  locSubscr = null;
  updateStatus();
}
btnStart.onClick.listen((Event e) {
  if (locSubscr == null) {
    bindListeners();
    updateStatus();
  }
});

btnStop.onClick.listen(cancelListeners);
}
```

The final app with a little CSS looks like this on iOS in Mobile Safari:

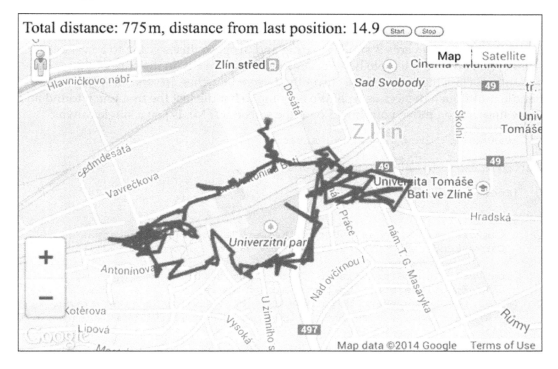

As you can see, the GPS location is quite inaccurate, so for the real usage, we would have to use a filter (for example, **the Kalman filter**) to reduce the position inaccuracy.

Calling pure JavaScript API from Dart isn't that hard, but it requires a little more surrounding code. We also saw that `JsObject` and `JsFunction` are sometimes replaceable. You can choose whether you want to use `JsObject.callMethod` or `JsFunction.apply`.

We also used `JsObject.jsify()` from the `dart:js` library that takes `List` or `Map` objects as parameters and converts them into `JsObject`, which is basically a wrapped JavaScript object.

Drawing into 2D canvas using onTouch events

Handling onTouch events is similar to drag and drop, so this is going to be very simple. Just one thing to note here: TouchEvent.touches is an instance of the TouchList class that contains all currently detected touches. In other words, you can handle multitouch devices as well. We're going to handle just the first touch found and draw lines as you move your finger over the screen. HTML is just a single canvas:

```
<canvas id="draw-canvas"></canvas>
```

Dart code listens to only two touch events:

```
import 'dart:html';

void main() {
  CanvasElement canvas = document.querySelector('#draw-canvas');
  CanvasRenderingContext2D context = canvas.getContext('2d');

  canvas.onTouchStart.listen((TouchEvent e) {
    // Move line start to the position where
    // the touch event began. We care only about the first touch.
    context.moveTo(e.touches[0].page.x, e.touches[0].page.y);
  });

  canvas.onTouchMove.listen((TouchEvent e) {
    context.lineWidth = 2;
    context.strokeStyle = "#FF0000";
    // Move a line to where I moved my finger.
    context.lineTo(e.touches[0].page.x, e.touches[0].page.y);
    // Draw the line.
    context.stroke();
  });

  // Set canvas size to documents size. With this, touch
  // coordinates will be the same as canvas coordinates.
  void resize() {
    canvas.width = document.body.client.width;
    canvas.height = document.body.client.height;
  }
  resize();
  // Add event listener on windows resize in order to have
  // always the canvas size equal to the windows size.
  window.onResize.listen((Event e) => resize());
}
```

Note that we resized the canvas to the size of the document. If we performed some demanding drawings, we could use a simple trick by setting `width` and `height` canvas attributes to, for example, half the document dimensions. This would make the canvas draw only half the size (that's one-fourth of the pixels than the original size) and then scale the result to fit entire canvas. This would speed up rendering a lot, but the final image would probably be a little blurry. The same effect is possible with CSS3's `scale` statement.

We can use Developer Tools to emulate mobile touch events just like we did with device rotation.

Summary

In this chapter, we took a look at some HTML5 APIs that are specific to mobile devices, although you can emulate them in a normal browser.

With CSS3 transformations, we can quite easily create simple 3D objects but they have their limitations and are suitable only in certain situations. They're definitely not a replacement for WebGL. Device orientation events and the GeoLocation API work in all modern mobile browsers, although they're not 100 percent compatible with desktop browsers.

The `dart:js` interoperation library can be used to proxy native JavaScript libraries such as the Google Maps API.

In the next chapter, we're going to start with polymer.dart. Polymer in JavaScript is an emerging technology developed by Google, which lets you create encapsulated reusable components and polymer.dart is its port to the Dart language. Components created with polymer.dart should be fully compatible with JavaScript Polymer in the long term.

5
Web Components and polymer.dart

Reusing independent components across multiple websites was always a bit painful up to now. You had to manually include CSS styles that can override your already existing styles, JavaScripts, copy and paste necessary HTML code, and usually in the end, write at least small JavaScripts.

For this reason, W3C is working on a specification called Web Components (http://webcomponents.org/). This is a set of standards that makes creating and reusing components very easy.

In the first part of this chapter, we'll take a look at what Web Components are and how they work in Dart while implementing one after another. We'll also quickly compare implementation in Dart and JavaScript.

In the second part, we're going to take a look at polymer.dart. Polymer is a JavaScript framework built on Web Components. Polymer.dart is its port to Dart. We'll use it for the bookshelf example from the previous chapter and see how it can help us write more encapsulated components for our web apps.

As Polymer is heavily based on Web Components, we'll set off with a brief exploration of each part of this standard.

Web Components

Web Components is a cutting-edge technology in development right now, and there still isn't complete native support by some browsers (Firefox, for example). It defines three major parts that are necessary to build and use isolated components: Shadow DOM, Custom Elements, and HTML Imports.

In addition, we'll use the `template` tag, which used to be part of the Web Components specification but has been moved to the HTML5 specification instead.

Shadow DOM

The basic problem with including third-party HTML and CSS into your page is that it's not encapsulated. Your CSS styles can modify included HTML elements and vice versa. This also includes overlapping element IDs, classes, and so on.

With Shadow DOM, you can create an encapsulated DOM tree, which is isolated from the rest of the DOM.

Custom Elements

The HTML specification contains a predefined number of tags that you can use. With Custom Elements, you can extend this set with your own tags that can contain HTML fragments and add functionality to it as you wish.

In combination with Shadow DOM, we can create custom tags that will contain an encapsulated DOM tree.

Template

Template is an HTML5 tag that can contain any HTML subtree and can be cloned in order to reuse its content multiple times.

An important distinction from just writing HTML structure into a hidden `<div>` element is that the HTML fragment inside `<template>` isn't used on page load. It's a DOM structure that is parsed by the browser but not processed, which means `<script>` doesn't run, audio/video doesn't play, and images don't load. You can't even query elements inside `<template>` with `document.getElementById()` or any other query selector.

With Templates, we can write content for our custom element just like any other HTML.

HTML Imports

HTML Imports extend existing `<link>` tags with the `rel="import"` attribute, which allows us to include HTML documents in other HTML documents and in combination with Shadow DOM, Custom Elements, and Templates, create completely independent components that can be included into any page with its full functionality by a single `<link>` tag.

 These four concepts combined represent the power and capabilities of Web Components.

You can see the current status of Web Components and read the editor's draft at `http://www.w3.org/standards/techs/components`.

The Web Components polyfill for older browsers

All parts of the Web Components specification aren't implemented across all of today's browsers, or else aren't enabled by default.

Chrome 36+ is fully capable of using Web Components by default (including Dartium). Firefox requires that you enable it manually. No matter what browser you're using, there's a polyfill that enables Web Components in most browsers (`https://github.com/WebComponents/webcomponentsjs`).

Dart Pub already contains this JavaScript library along with a small script that is required when using the compiled version from `dart2js`. Add `web_components` to your dependencies and include the polyfill JavaScripts in your page:

```
<script src="packages/web_components/webcomponents.js"></script>
<script src="packages/web_components/dart_support.js"></script>
```

For an up-to-date status about the browser compatibility, refer to `http://caniuse.com/`.

Basic HTML Import

Time to see an HTML Import in action! Let's say we want to reuse this little greeting among multiple pages:

```
<!-- web/greeting.html -->
<div>
  <h1>Hello, imported world!</h1>
</div>
```

Now, insert it, for example, at the end of the body on this page (the following code). Note that CORS rules apply to imported HTML documents just as we saw in *Chapter 3, The Power of HTML5 with Dart*:

```
<!-- web/index.html -->
<html>
  <head>
    <!-- Polyfill for browsers not supporting Web Components. -->
    <script src="packages/web_components/webcomponents.js">
    </script>

    <link id="linkedCont" rel="import" href="greeting.html">

    <script type="application/dart" src="main.dart"></script>
    <script src="packages/browser/dart.js"></script>
  </head>
  <body>
    <!-- Insert greeting here. -->
  </body>
</html>
```

This HTML just loads our greeting into a separate DOM tree. To append its content into our page, we need to write some Dart code:

```
// web/main.dart
import 'dart:html';

void main() {
  LinkElement cont = document.querySelector('#linkedCont');
  // Notice that we can select any DOM element and clone
  // only it and its subtree (true = deep copy).
  var cloned = cont.import.querySelector('div').clone(true);

  document.body.append(cloned);
}
```

LinkElement has the import property, which is an instance of the Document class itself, just like the top-level document variable from the dart:html package. Then, select div from the imported document, clone it, and append it to the page.

Let's see the structure this created in the browser:

This is what we expected. The linked `greeting.html` HTML document has it's own DOM subtree that we can access through the `import` property, and then clone what we want.

We can modify `greeting.html` and add some CSS styles to it:

```
<!-- web/greeting.html -->
<style>
h1 { color: red; }
h2 { color: green; }
</style>
<div>
  <h1>Hello, imported world!</h1>
</div>
```

Also, add another heading inside the body of our page:

```
<body>
  <h2>Greeting here</h2>
  <!-- Insert greeting here -->
</body>
```

Then, let's see what happens:

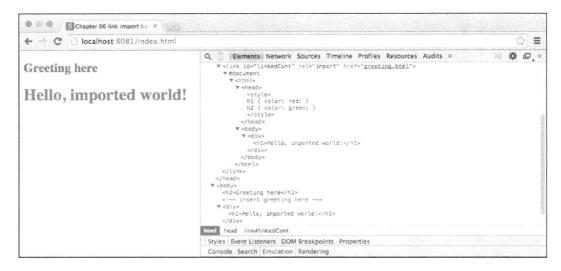

Although we cloned just the `div` element containing the `<h1>` heading, styles from the linked HTML document are applied to all HTML elements on the page. This is probably not what we wanted and it shows that just including HTML using the `<link>` tag isn't enough. We need to encapsulate included HTML and CSS styles.

We need the Shadow DOM!

Using Shadow DOM

As we want to apply styles from `greeting.html` only to elements in `greeting.html`, we'll wrap it with HTML5 Template. As we mentioned earlier in this chapter, everything inside the `<template>` tag will get parsed into DOM elements but won't be run. This means that styles inside `<template>` have no effect until we paste them outside of the template:

```
<!-- web/greeting.html -->
<template>
  <style>
  h1 { color: blue; }
  h2 { color: yellow; }
  </style>
  <h1>Hello, imported world!</h1>
</template>
```

In order to make it more like a real-world example, we'll add some styles to `index.html` as well:

```html
<!-- index.html -->
<head>
  <link rel="import" href="greeting.html" id="myElementLink">
  <style>
  h1 { color: red !important }
  h2 { color: green; }
  </style>
</head>
<body>
  <h2>Greeting here</h2>
  <!-- Insert greeting here. -->
  <!-- We'll create Shadow DOM in this element. -->
  <div></div>
</body>
```

We first colored `<h1>` red and then blue in the imported HTML. Then, we colored `<h2>` green and yellow, respectively. The question is, what colors will `<h1>` and `<h2>` have inside the body?

Now, let's update the Dart code. Instead of pasting cloned elements from the imported document right into the top-level document body, we'll create a Shadow DOM and paste it inside this new so-called shadow-root:

```dart
// web/main.dart
import 'dart:html';

void main() {
  LinkElement cont = document.querySelector('#myElementLink');
  var template = cont.import.querySelector('template');
  // Get DOM subtree from the external document,
  // clone it and make it available in the current document.
  Node clone = template.content.clone(true);
  // Target element where we'll put cloned elements.
  DivElement targetDiv = document.querySelector('body > div');
  // Create a Shadow DOM in the target element and insert
  // the cloned elements inside the new root.
  ShadowRoot root = targetDiv.createShadowRoot();
  root.append(clone);
}
```

So, what are the colors of `<h1>` and `<h2>` now? Take a look:

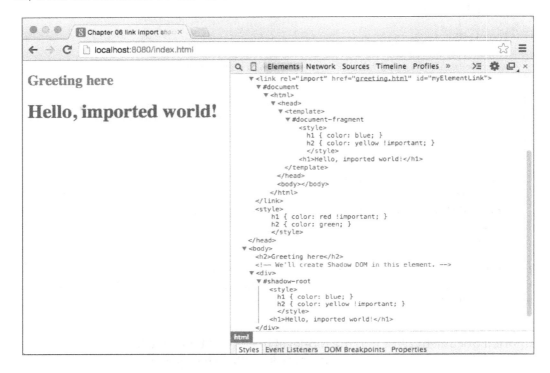

As shown in the preceding screenshot, `<h1>` is blue. The root document's styles don't apply to it because `<h1>` is inside the Shadow DOM, which has its own styles, and those color `<h1>` blue. The logic behind the `<h2>` color is analogous. Our `<div>` target, where we placed the cloned DOM subtree from the imported template, has turned into a document itself.

This is nice, but we still have to clone the elements by ourselves; with a more complicated DOM structure, we would have to add classes to the elements that we want to replace with our custom templates. Also, when adding DOM elements dynamically, we have to first add them to the DOM tree and then replace them using Dart, as we did right now.

That's all doable, but it's a bit clumsy.

Using Custom Elements

For this reason, Web Components have Custom Elements. We're going to define a custom tag called `<my-greeting>` that the browser will automatically replace with our template—just like any other tag in HTML.

Our `greeting.html` file will include one extra element, selectable by ID, that will be customizable by one of the element's attribute. The same ID will be used in every instance of `<my-greeting>` that is correct and doesn't collide because each element instance has it's own Shadow DOM:

```
<!-- web/greeting.html -->
<template>
  <style>
  h1 { color: yellow; }
  h2 { color: red; }
  </style>

  <h2>Template</h2>
  <p id="content">Lorem ipsum</p>
</template>
```

The body for `index.html` is going to be even simpler than before:

```
<body>
  <h2>Hello, world!</h2>
  <button>Add</button>
  <my-greeting></my-greeting>
  <my-greeting custom-attribute="Hello"></my-greeting>
</body>
```

The Dart code will be mostly the same as the previous example. We'll just wrap the elements' configuration into a class that extends Dart's `HtmlElement` class. Note that you can extend any existing class that already extends `HtmlElement` or `SvgElement`:

```
// web/main.dart
import 'dart:html';

class MyGreetingElement extends HtmlElement {
  // The created() constructor is called every time
  // the tag is instantiated and calls parent's constructor first.
  MyGreetingElement.created() : super.created() {
    LinkElement cont = document.querySelector('#myElementLink');
    TemplateElement template =
        cont.import.querySelector('template');

    // Get DOM subtree from the external document,
    // clone it and make it available in the current document.
    Node clone = document.importNode(template.content, true);

    // Create a Shadow DOM in the target element and insert
```

```
        // cloned elements inside the shadow-root.
        ShadowRoot root = this.createShadowRoot();
        root.append(clone);

        // Check if this element has this attribute set.
        if (this.attributes.containsKey('custom-attribute')) {
          // Root is an encapsulated document created
          // for this instance.
          root.querySelector('#content').text =
              this.attributes['custom-attribute'];
        }
    }

    // Redefine the default constructor
    // This lets us use just "new MyGreetingElement()" to
    // create new instances.
    factory MyGreetingElement() => new Element.tag('my-greeting');
}

void main() {
    // Let the browser know that we have our own element under
    // this tag name.
    document.registerElement('my-greeting', MyGreetingElement);

    // Allow user to dynamically add more elements.
    document.querySelector('button').onClick.listen((e) {
      document.querySelector('body')
          .children.add(new MyGreetingElement());
    });
}
```

We're using **Factory design pattern** and the `factory` keyword because we want this constructor to return an instance of a different class than `MyGreetingElement`. Subclasses of `HtmlElement` can't use the default constructor because new instances have to be created using the named constructor `HtmlElement.created()`.

The most interesting part here is the `document.registerElement()` method, which tells the browser that the `<my-greeting>` tag is going to be an instance of `MyGreetingElement` and will instantiate it using the `MyGreetingElement.created()` constructor.

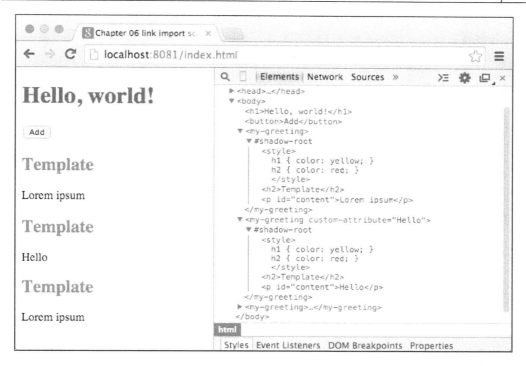

This is already quite useful. We have a custom tag that we can easily, dynamically instantiate. It's nice, but it's not an independent component that you can just include on your page with a single `<link>` tag and start using custom tags right away. We still have to call `document.registerElement()` manually.

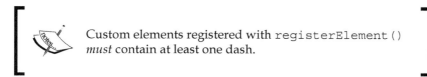

Custom elements registered with `registerElement()` *must* contain at least one dash.

In vanilla JavaScript, we can register a custom element right from the imported document:

```
<!-- greeting.html with JavaScript -->
<template>
  <style>
  h1 { color: yellow; }
  h2 { color: red; }
  </style>

  <h2>Template</h2>
  <p id="content">Lorem ipsum</p>
```

```
</template>
<script type="text/javascript">
(function() {
  // var importDoc = document.currentScript.ownerDocument;
  // Listen to the createdCallback event and
  // register this tag in the root document automatically.
  // document.registerElement(...);
})();
</script>
```

The JavaScript inside `<script>` tags gets executed right after the browser loads it because it's outside the `<template>` tag.

Unfortunately, we can't do this in Dart due to Dart's embedding policies:

- Only one Dart script is allowed per document

- Dart doesn't support inline scripts (you can't write scripts inside HTML)

- For more information about these restrictions, refer to `https://www.dartlang.org/articles/embedding-in-html`

Also, changes to custom attributes of our `<my-greeting>` tag aren't projected to the Shadow DOM automatically. This means that if you modified `custom-attribute` dynamically, it wouldn't change the text inside the `#content` paragraph because we set the text just once in its constructor.

One option is to listen to change events with `MutationObserver`:

```
void onMutation(List<MutationRecord> mut, MutationObserver ob) {
  // Handle changes.
};
MutationObserver observer = new MutationObserver(onMutation);
observer.observe(root.querySelector('#content').parent);
```

But we're not going to go into it here.

If you really wanted to do this by yourself, or had some very specific needs, check out the `Observe` library (`https://pub.dartlang.org/packages/observe`). This is used internally by polymer.dart and we'll use it in a moment.

Remember that you can make use of each part of Web Components separately even without diving into Polymer or Angular. For example, when you include a new JavaScript library into your existing project that overrides your styles, or that unnecessarily manipulates elements with its JavaScript code and you don't like it, you can use the Shadow DOM and Templates to isolate it from the rest of the page.

Polymer.dart

Polymer.dart is a port of the JavaScript Polymer library that combines Web Components, the Observe library, and a few others libraries into a single framework. This makes creating reusable encapsulated components very easy (it also uses polymer.js internally).

As we already know enough about Web Components, we'll particularly take a look at one-way / two-way data binding and creating custom elements with their behavior written in Dart.

> You might have already seen Dart's Web UI package used in a tutorial, blog, article, or a book. Web UI is an older Dart API, which is deprecated in favor of polymer.dart.

Minimalistic custom element in polymer.dart

We'll begin by installing polymer.dart by adding polymer among our dependencies in pubspec.yaml and letting Dart Editor fetch all the dependencies for us. Right away, we can tell polymer.dart what our app's entrance points are. These are the pages that the user can access (that's probably everything except HTML templates for our custom elements), so all our pubspec.yaml files will look alike. When compiling apps with Pub Build, this also lets polymer.dart concatenate all pages together for faster loading:

```
name: Chapter_05_polymer_tutorial
description: My first Polymer app
dependencies:
  browser: any
  polymer: '>=0.16.0 <0.17.0'
transformers:
- polymer:
    entry_points: web/index.html
```

The HTML for index.html is going to be very simple and mostly what we've already seen in the previous examples. Note that we're including the Dart script at the end. It has to be included after importing custom elements, so the best practice is to put it at the end:

```
<!-- web/index.html -->
<html>
  <head>
    <script src="packages/browser/dart.js"></script>
    <link rel="import" href="my-element.html">
  </head>
```

```
<body>
  <my-element></my-element>
  <script type="application/dart" src="main.dart"></script>
</body>
</html>
```

Where things start to get interesting is with our element's definition in `my-element.html`. Each custom element in polymer.dart has to be in a separate file that imports the Polymer stub code at the top and contains one `<polymer-element>` tag. The `<polymer-element>` is a wrapper for our custom element that can use:

- **The HTML template**: This is required for all custom elements.

- **CSS styles (optional)**: Use this to style only the Shadow DOM encapsulated from the rest of the page. There's a special CSS `:host` keyword that refers to the current `host` element. We'll see this in action later.

- **Dart script (optional)**: This is your custom code that defines the element's behavior.

To keep it very simple, we'll create a custom element that contains only the HTML template with no styles and no Dart:

```
<!-- lib/my-element.html -->
<link rel="import" href="../packages/polymer/polymer.html">
<polymer-element name="my-element" noscript>
  <template>
    <h1>Hello polymer.dart!</h1>
  </template>
</polymer-element>
```

Each custom element has to import `polymer.html` before declaring the element itself. The `polymer.html` file comes from the JavaScript Polymer project and is part of the polymer.dart package. For larger components with multiple files, you might want to look at directory structure recommendations at `https://www.dartlang.org/polymer/app-directories.html`.

As polymer.dart expects that your custom element will have some Dart attached to it by default, we have to tell it specifically that this element has no script with the `noscript` attribute.

Our element's name is going to be `my-element` (the name *has to* contain at least one dash, just like in the previous example).

The last part, for now, is `main.dart`, which will initialize `polymer.dart`:

```
// web/main.dart
import 'package:polymer/polymer.dart';

main() async {
  // Recommended way of running main() with polymer.dart
  // [initPolymer()] returns a Future object that is completed
  // when all imports are loaded. New since polymer.dart 0.16.
  (await initPolymer()).run(() {
    // The rest of the code in the main method.
  });
}
```

This may look weird at first sight. The code for `main()` should be in a callback to the `run()` method of `initPolymer()`. This makes use of the so-called Zone-related API, which is like a unified way of handling exceptions from asynchronous calls. It's not important for us, but if you want to read more about this topic, check out `https://www.dartlang.org/articles/zones/`.

Now, we can run our first polymer.dart application:

We can see that polymer.dart did pretty much the same as what we did with vanilla Web Components. It created a Shadow DOM and cloned the content of the `<template>` to `<my-element>`.

But there's already an important difference. We didn't have to write any code specific to this custom element. Everything is done for us in the background by polymer.dart.

Polymer examples in this chapter use polymer.dart version 0.16 that uses Polymer 0.5 internally, which is just a developer preview.

One-way data binding

Creating new elements is easy, but without any logic behind them, it isn't very practical. We've already said that polymer.dart utilizes the Observe library, which we can use to listen to changes of attributes on element instances and also to create one-way data bindings, which we'll use now.

Our new custom element will be called `<one-way-book>`, and we'll reuse the 3D books that we created in *Chapter 4, Developing a Mobile App with Dart*. Just to present polymer's capabilities, we'll add two control buttons that will rotate each book, and a caption of the book floating above them with the name of its current cover image.

The body for this example will look very familiar. We'll just add two elements with two custom attributes that we'll use later in Dart code:

```
<!-- web/index.html -->
<body>
  <one-way-book cover-image="./dune-cover-new.jpg"
        base-color="#da944c"></one-way-book>
  <one-way-book cover-image="./dune-cover-old.jpg"
        base-color="#000"></one-way-book>
</body>
```

The HTML template is going to be slightly more complicated with a few new features:

```
<!-- lib/one-way-book.html -->
<link rel="import" href="../packages/polymer/polymer.html">
<polymer-element name="one-way-book">
  <template>
    <style>
     /* This refers to the host element. */
    :host { display: inline-block; position: relative;
            transform-style: preserve-3d; margin: 20px; }
    div { transform-style: preserve-3d; }
    div > div { width: 150px; height: 230px; position: absolute; }
     /* This is the same like in Chapter 4. */
    </style>

    <div>
```

```
        <p id="name">{{coverImage}}<br />{{rotateYString}}</p>
        <div class="front"
            style="background-image:url({{coverImage}})"></div>
        <div class="left"></div>
        <div class="right"></div>
        <div class="back"></div>
        <div class="top"></div>
        <div class="bottom"></div>
      </div>

      <p id="buttons">
        <!-- Buttons with event listeners. -->
        <button on-click="{{rotateLeft}}">&lt; left</button>
        <button on-click="{{rotateRight}}">right &gt;</button>
      </p>
    </template>
    <!-- Dart script that will control this custom element. -->
    <script type="application/dart"
        src="one-way-book.dart"></script>
</polymer-element>
```

As you can see, there are two unusual things:

- `{{coverImage}}` and `{{rotateYString}}`: These are notations that render instance properties to this place in an HTML document. The associated property has to be marked with the `@observe` annotation. This is the one-way data binding that we mentioned earlier. Changes to the variable in the Dart code will automatically update the rendered value in HTML.

- `on-click`: This is a declarative event mapping that is used to bind events right into the HTML. When the event is triggered, polymer.dart will call only the listener associated with this particular element's instance. There are more types of events, such as `on-change` (for input elements) or `on-tap`.

 Note that we're using `{{coverImage}}` in two different places — first as a text inside <p> tag and then right inside the `style` attribute of a `div` element, in order to avoid setting this style manually in the Dart code.

We'll start the Dart code with just a class stub:

```
// lib/one-way-book.dart
// Associate this class with the tag name.
// Each instance of <one-way-book> will be
// controlled by an instance of OneWayBookElement.
@CustomTag('one-way-book')
```

```
class OneWayBookElement extends PolymerElement {

  // This property can be embedded in the HTML by {{coverImage}}.
  @observable String coverImage;

  // Constructor is called every time a new instance is created.
  OneWayBookElement.created() : super.created() {
    // ...
  }

  attributeChanged(String name, String old, String newVal) {}
  rotateLeft(Event e, var detail, Node target) { }
  // ...
}
```

Our custom element extends `PolymerElement`, but it can extend any HTML element that implements `Polymer` and `Observable` abstract classes and provides the `MyElement.created()` constructor that calls `super.created()`.

Elements in polymer.dart have five life cycle methods:

- `CustomElement.created()`: This constructor is used when creating a new instance of this element
- `attached()`: This instance is inserted into the DOM
- `detached()`: This instance is removed from the DOM
- `ready()`: This is called when the Shadow DOM is created, event listeners and properties are binded
- `attributeChanged()`: This is called every time an attribute is changed, removed, or added to the element

This is the complete source code with comments:

```
// lib/one-way-book.dart
import 'dart:html';
import 'package:polymer/polymer.dart';

@CustomTag('one-way-book')
class OneWayBookElement extends PolymerElement {

  // These properties can be embedded in the HTML.
  @observable String coverImage;
  @observable String rotateYString;
  int rotateY = 0;
```

```dart
  void updateBaseColor(String newColor) {
    // Btw, shadowRoot.host refers to the host element itself.
    shadowRoot.querySelector('.left').style.background = newColor;
    shadowRoot.querySelector('.back').style.background = newColor;
  }

  // Constructor called every time a new instance is created.
  OneWayBookElement.created() : super.created() {
    coverImage = this.attributes['cover-image'];
    updateBaseColor(this.attributes['base-color']);
  }

  // Listen to all attribute changes.
  void attributeChanged(String name, String old, String newVal) {
    super.attributeChanged(name, oldValue, newValue);
    print('$name: $newValue (old $oldValue)');
    // base-color attribute has been changed.
    if (name == 'base-color') {
      this.updateBaseColor(newValue);
    } else if (name == 'cover-image') {
      // Note that we don't need to change cover-image manually
      // since this property is embedded right in the HTML it'll
      // update automatically.
      coverImage = newValue;
    }
  }

  // Event listeners triggered on button clicks.
  void rotateLeft(Event e, var detail, Node target) {
    rotateY -= 10;
    updateRotation();
  }

  void rotateRight(Event e, var detail, Node target) {
    rotateY += 10;
    updateRotation();
  }

  void updateRotation() {
    rotateYString = 'rotateY(${rotateY}deg)';
    var elm = shadowRoot.querySelector('div');
    elm.style.transform = rotateYString;
  }
}
```

The `main.dart` file is the same as the one in the previous example.

What happens in the browser is obvious. Clicking on one of the buttons calls their binded methods in their instance of `OneWayBookElement`, which changes CSS3 transformations in the `rotateYString` property. Each change to this variable updates all its bindings in the HTML.

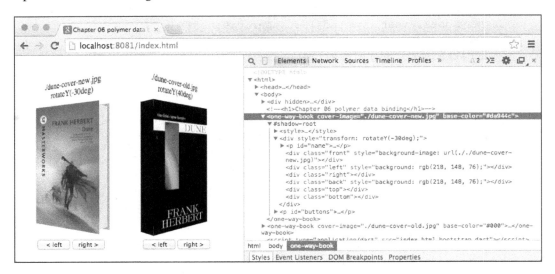

To test whether changing the element's attributes really triggers `attributeChanged()`, we can use Developer Tools right in Dartium. Just double-click on, for example, the `base-color` attribute to anything you want, and you can see that each change is immediately propagated to the element's instance in Dart. You can try changing the `cover-image` attribute as well.

Instead of the `@observable` annotation, we could use `@published` for `coverImage` that watches the property for changes (just like `@observable`) and also binds the element's attribute of this name with this property. This is nice when you don't need any additional logic when attribute values change.

Loops and conditions in templates

Polymer.dart comes with custom attributes `if` and `repeat`, which can evaluate simple logic useful mostly to hide and show DOM subtrees. We could use it, for example, to hide the book title with the rotation and image name when the rotation is larger than 30 degrees:

```
// lib/one-way-book.dart
// Declare rotateY in OneWayBookElement class.
@observable int rotateY = 0;

<!-- lib/one-way-book.html -->
<div>
  <template if="{{ rotateY < 30 && rotateY > -30 }}">
    <p id="name">{{ coverImage }}<br />{{ rotateYString }}</p>
  </template>
</div>
```

When the condition inside the `if` attribute evaluates to `true`, its inner subtree is placed in the parent element at the same location where the `<template>` tag is used.

Similarly, with the `repeat` attribute, we can iterate a collection. For example, if we had both book covers in a list called `booksCovers`, we could render them with:

```
<template repeat="{{ image in booksCovers }}">
  <one-way-book cover-image="{{ image }}" base-color="#000">
  </one-way-book>
</template>
```

Data binding applies to all expressions, so changing any variable will automatically cause reevaluation of the entire expression.

Two-way data binding

Now, we'll take a look at two-way data binding, which usually goes hand-in-hand with forms.

In one-way data binding, we embedded the instance's property into the HTML template. The direction went only from the instance to the HTML.

But with form input fields, we can propagate its values from the HTML input to instance properties and back to HTML. In other words, you can change the instance's property by changing the input value, but you can also change the input value by changing the instance's property. This is why it's called two-way binding.

Better still, let's create an example. We'll create a page that includes the `<my-form>` custom element:

```
<!-- web/index.html -->
<html>
  <head>
    <script async src="packages/browser/dart.js"></script>
    <link rel="import" href="my-form.html">
  </head>
  <body>
    <my-form></my-form>
    <script type="application/dart" src="main.dart"></script>
  </body>
</html>
```

In this case, our custom element is a small form:

```
<!-- lib/my-form.html -->
<link rel="import" href="../packages/polymer/polymer.html">
<polymer-element name="my-form">
  <template>
    <form>
      <h3>input value {{inputValue}}</h3>
      <input type="range" value={{inputValue}}>
      <button type="button" on-click="{{set50}}">set 50</button>
    </form>
  </template>
  <script type="application/dart" src="my_form.dart"></script>
</polymer-element>
```

Note that we're embedding `inputValue` into two places and also binding an event called `set50()`. Setting `inputValue` as a parameter to the `value` attribute means that every change to the input's value will propagate to the `inputValue` property:

```
// lib/my_form.dart
import 'dart:html';
import 'package:polymer/polymer.dart';

@CustomTag('my-form')
class MyFormElement extends PolymerElement {

  @observable String inputValue = '0';
```

```
    MyFormElement.created() : super.created();

    void set50(Event e, var detail, Node target) {
      inputValue = '50';
    }
  }
```

We are setting `inputValue` by the `<input>` element, but at the same time, you can change its value by clicking on the button. The question is, will pressing the button and setting `inputValue` to `50` also change the input element? Yes, it will, because it's making use of two-way data binding.

We will use two-way data binding again in the next chapter with AngularDart.

Polymer core and paper elements

Google Polymer team is maintaining numerous Polymer elements ranging from custom image placeholders, menus, tooltips, tabs, to inputs fields. All of them with unified look and feel. Although, their practical usage is questionable apart from making prototypes, one of them stands out particularly.

A quick look at core-list

Core-list is a Polymer component designed for rendering a very large amount of elements in a list (thousands without any problem). It internally creates only those elements that are visible to the user and as they scroll, it positions them absolutely to users viewport with CSS3 transformations (the same transformations that we used in *Chapter 4*, *Developing a Mobile App with Dart*).

We'll create a new project, add `polymer` and `core-elements` dependencies and then create a custom element with our entire app that generates 1 million of random colors and render them into one large list:

```
// lib/main_app.dart
import 'dart:math';
import 'package:polymer/polymer.dart';

@CustomTag('main-app')
class MainApp extends PolymerElement {
  Random _rnd;

  // ObservableList is a Polymer class that emits events when
  // items in the list change. It's required by <core-list>.
  @observable ObservableList largeList = new ObservableList();

  MainApp.created() : super.created() {
    _rnd = new Random();
    for (int i = 0; i < pow(10, 6); i++) {
      largeList.add([getRandomColor()]);
    }
  }

  String getRandomColor() =>
      _colorComp() + _colorComp() + _colorComp();
  String _colorComp() =>
      _rnd.nextInt(256).toRadixString(16).padLeft(2, '0');
}
```

Then write HTML template for our app. Polymer's `<core-list>` automatically generates **index** and **model** variables for us, which represent the current item's index and the current item itself respectively.

```
<link rel="import" href="../../packages/polymer/polymer.html">
<link rel="import"
    href="../../packages/core_elements/core_list_dart.html">
<polymer-element name="main-app">
  <template>
    <style>
    #list { height: 100%; }
    #list div { padding: 3px; }
    </style>

    <core-list-dart id="list" data="{{largeList}}">
      <template>
        <div>
```

```
        <span>#{{index}}: </span>
        <span style="color:#{{model}}">Hello, World!</span>
      </div>
    </template>
  </core-list-dart>
</template>
<script type="application/dart" src="main_app.dart"></script>
</polymer-element>
```

Polymer's `<core-list>` element replicates its inner `<template>` tag and interpolates all values in it. We can check which HTML elements core-list generated for us:

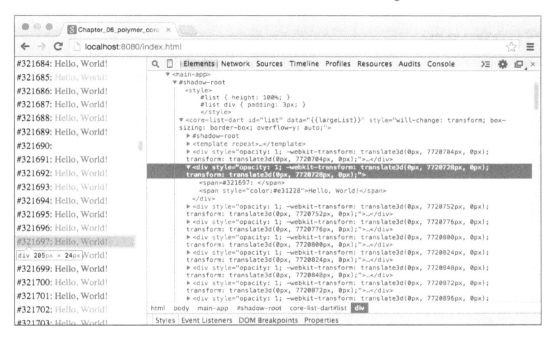

Although we're rendering a list with 1 million items, there are only about 40 `div` elements actually created and reused as you scroll (it also created `div` elements that are around your current viewport). Note that it doesn't wrap itself nor rendered items with Shadow DOM because that would prevent you from styling it with CSS. Core-list speeds up rendering large lists enormously and works on both desktop and mobile browsers.

What's next?

Polymer.dart can offer even more. We're not able to cover everything here, so we have to leave it up to your curiosity, but we hope you have an idea what polymer. dart is good for, and in what kind of situations you can use it.

For a more comprehensive list of tutorials, check out the port of Polymer tutorials from JavaScript into Dart at `https://github.com/dart-lang/polymer-dart-patterns` and the official polymer.dart documentation at `https://www.dartlang.org/polymer/`.

Summary

This chapter covered Web Components and polymer.dart. Each topic is so vast that it could easily cover the entire book. Here, we explained the most important parts, so you should now understand how these technologies work in a nutshell.

Web Components are useful even without Polymer and you can use parts of it independently even now with polyfills for older browsers.

Polymer.dart is built on top of Web Components and adds very nifty things to it.

In the next chapter, we'll talk about AngularDart, where you'll find many features already familiar from polymer.dart.

6
AngularDart

AngularDart is a client-side framework used to create structured decoupled web applications using the **Model-View-Controller** (**MVC**) design pattern. Angular currently exists in two languages, JavaScript and Dart. Both projects are developed by Google and share the same philosophy, although their implementation is fundamentally different.

In this chapter, we'll learn how to use AngularDart to create two applications, and you'll see that we are already familiar with many things from the previous chapter that covered polymer.dart:

- **To-do list**: With two-way data binding and a couple of Angular directives, we can create tedious tasks such as creating/removing DOM elements very easily
- **Book component**: We'll reuse the book template from *Chapter 4*, *Developing a Mobile App with Dart*, once more and compare polymer.dart and AngularDart implementations

At the end of this chapter, we'll make a few notes about performance bottlenecks when using AngularDart, and what you can do about them.

 If you already have previous experience with AngularJS, you'll find many things in this chapter familiar, although even for developers new to the Angular world, this chapter should be easy to understand.

We won't be able to go through every single aspect of AngularDart. Just like AngularJS, it could easily fill an entire book, so we'll rather focus on the most interesting parts and how they relate to what we already know.

AngularDart encourages you to use MVC. In this case, the letter "C" is meant as a component instead of a controller, as you're probably more used to.

Officially, Angular follows **MVW**, which means **Model-View-Whatever**. Seriously. Angular was closer to MVC in the past; now it's closer to MVVM. Igor Minar, an AngularJS developer at Google, stated this on G+ after being tired of never-ending and pointless discussions among developers as to what design pattern Angular follows. So, he called it MVW because it doesn't matter (https://plus.google.com/+AngularJS/posts/aZNVhj355G2).

To see all AngularDart features, refer to its documentation at https://docs.angulardart.org/.

Installing AngularDart

Just like polymer.dart, the simplest way to install AngularDart is by adding it to your pubspec.yaml file:

```
name: todo_list
version: 0.0.1
description: My first AngularDart app
dependencies:
  angular: 1.1.0
  browser: any
  web_components: any
transformers:
- angular
```

Note that we had to add angular to the transformers directive as well. This tells the pub tool that there are some extra tasks defined in AngularDart libraries. Even if you're used to adding dependencies in Dart Editor's GUI, you still have to add the transformer yourself.

AngularDart reached version 1.1.0 and is still in development. All examples in this chapter are using this version.

To-do list with AngularDart

We'll set off with quite a simple application, where you can dynamically add tasks to a list and then gradually extend it with more complex functionality, while showing the most common AngularDart features.

We'll keep the HTML code very simple:

```
<!-- web/index.html -->
<html ng-app>
<body>
  <todo-list></todo-list>

  <script type="application/dart" src="main.dart"></script>
  <script src="packages/browser/dart.js"></script>
</body>
</html>
```

Note the `ng-app` directive inside the `<html>` tag. This tells AngularDart that everything inside this DOM tree is controlled by Angular. In practice, this means that you shouldn't modify the DOM tree by yourself and leave all DOM manipulations to Angular; otherwise, this might cause unpredictable behavior. Also, we're including the Web Components polyfill that we already know from the previous chapter. You can probably guess that AngularDart is going to use Web Components.

 If you don't set `ng-app` by yourself, it'll be set by AngularDart to root `<html>` tag by default, so we'll omit it in future examples.

Now, we define `<todo-list>` custom element. Right now, it's going be just a single Dart class:

```
// lib/component/todo_list.dart
import 'package:angular/angular.dart';

// Mark class as Component with annotation.
@Component(
    selector: 'todo-list', // CSS selector for this component
    template: """
      <h1>{{ title }}</h1>
      <ul>
        <li ng-repeat="task in tasks">{{ task }}</li>
      </ul>
    """ // Multiline string as a template.
)
```

```
class TodoListComponent {
  String title = "My Todo list";

  // Default tasks.
  List<String> tasks = [
    "Buy more cat food",
    "Feed the cat",
    "Do the laundry",
  ];
}
```

There are already a few interesting parts. `@Component` is an annotation that tells AngularDart that this class has a special meaning. It offers a few possible options:

- `selector`: This tells AngularDart how to find elements that are going to be replaced by this component. Note that the selector is a CSS expression. This means that you can select an element just as in CSS, for example, `#my-element` or `.my-element`: although it's recommended that you use element names as selectors.

- `template` or `templateUrl`: As our component is very simple, we can just include the template as a string, which is okay when it's relatively short. With larger HTML templates, it's much easier to read and maintain code in a separate HTML file. We'll do this in a moment.

- `cssUrl`: Every component is encapsulated in a Shadow DOM, so the CSS from the parent document doesn't apply to its elements. Therefore, you can provide your component with a custom CSS file. We already saw this in the previous chapter, when we talked about Web Components and polymer.dart.

- `useShadowDom`: By default, AngularDart encapsulates each component with the Shadow DOM, which is usually fine, but if you know that this particular component is going to be used many times on your page, you might want to disable creating the Shadow DOM for each of them for performance reasons (encapsulation is then emulated by AngularDart).

- `exportExpressions`: More on this will be covered later in this chapter.

Let's take a better look at the template:

```
<h1>{{ title }}</h1>
<ul>
  <li ng-repeat="task in tasks">{{ task }}</li>
</ul>
```

AngularDart uses double curly braces, aka mustache syntax {{ expression }} (just like polymer.dart), to interpolate results of expressions in a Dart-like syntax. It has two limitations:

- No flow control statements are allowed. This means that there are no ifs or loops; only ternary operators are allowed: (boolExpr ? yesExpp : noExpr). Expressions can contain the + sign to concatenate strings. For example, {{ "Hello" + "World" }} will print HelloWorld.

- When dereferencing objects such as my.object.property, any of them in the chain can be null and Dart won't throw any exception.

In our template, we call {{ title }}, which prints the current content of TodoListComponent.title. The {{ title }} expression is automatically watched by Angular for changes, so if you modify title on the run, it will be immediately re-rendered in the template (AngularDart is using two-way data binding similarly to what we've already used in polymer.dart).

Angular built-in ng-* directives allow you to alter the element's behavior in some way. In this template, we have only one:

- ng-repeat: This iterates all elements, such as "item in collection" and clones the parent element for each item in the collection. In our example, all items in the task list are instances of Dart's string, so we can just print them. We'll come back to this directive later.

The last thing is main.dart, which just connects all parts together:

```
// web/main.dart
import 'package:angular/angular.dart';
import 'package:angular/application_factory.dart';
// We're expecting that our component is
// reusable across many applications.
import 'package:todo_list/component/todo_list.dart';

class MyAppModule extends Module {
  MyAppModule() {
    // Enable our component in this app.
    bind(TodoListComponent);
  }
}

void main() {
```

```
    // Bootstrap code for AngularDart.
    applicationFactory()
        // Add our module among default AngularDart modules.
        .addModule(new MyAppModule())
        .run();
}
```

Note that we're importing `todo_list.dart` like any other package (our app is a package too) because we're expecting that our component is going to be reusable and independent on this application. The same applied to polymer.dart in the previous chapter.

AngularDart uses the **dependency injection** pattern under the hood, which means that it only instantiates classes that you actually use in your code (thus saving resources), and allows you to reuse components and modules that have dependencies by themselves, without you worrying about the order of imports. Our application is a single module with just one component.

The directory structure for this app should look like this:

 The directory structure that we're using here is recommended for packages and projects using AngularDart.

When you run this application in the browser, you'll see:

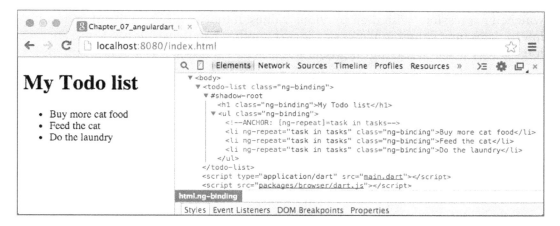

AngularDart created the Shadow DOM for our custom element, filled it with the template, and cloned `<li>` elements for each item in the `TodoListComponent.tasks` list.

 This is one of the implementation differences from AngularJS. AngularJS 1.x doesn't use Web Components when creating custom elements and it doesn't encapsulate them inside the Shadow DOM, while AngularDart does. After all, using Web Components is planed for Angular 2.0.

At the beginning of this chapter, we said that AngularDart is based on MVC. Let's see how each part of MVC is represented in our application:

- **Component**: As our app is very simple, we have only the `TodoListComponent`. But it's a standalone component that has its own template and its own logic independent on the application using it.
- **View**: Our view is our template with interpolated variables from the model.
- **Model**: We have two model variables in this example, `title` and `tasks`. In the Angular world, all model variables exist in a scope.

Scope

In Angular, a **scope** is a context that evaluates expressions. You can imagine it as a scope in JavaScript that keeps track of expressions and watches for changes. Scopes can be nested, usually with a similar structure, such as your DOM tree where the root scope is defined by the `ng-app` directive.

When you trigger an Angular event (such as `ng-click` or `ng-input`, which we'll show later), Angular first runs your handler and then checks the current values of all watched expressions with their previous values. If they're different, it automatically interpolates new values in views or triggers another handlers (this can cause an infinite loop when used improperly).

Some Angular directives such as `ng-repeat` or `ng-if` create child scopes for their subtrees, which might cause performance bottlenecks when used too much. We will talk about some performance optimization tips at the end of this chapter.

In our app, the scope is filled by AngularDart automatically and watches `"title"`, `"task in tasks"`, and `"task"` expressions. This means that if you alter the `tasks` list, it will automatically recreate the DOM structure inside the `<ul>` element.

Now we'll extend this application with more `ng-*` directives, put templates into separate HTML files, and add simple routing.

Extending the to-do list

We can keep `index.html` as is and start by adding routing to our `main.dart` file:

```
// web/main.dart
moduleRouteInitializer(Router router, RouteViewFactory views) {
  views.configure({
    // This route will be displayed even when no path is set.
    'add': ngRoute(
        defaultRoute: true,
        path: '/add',
        view: 'view/add.html'),
    // Detail of a task identified by its id.
    'detail': ngRoute(
        path: '/detail/:taskId',
        view: 'view/detail.html'),
  });
}

class MyAppModule extends Module {
  MyAppModule() {
    bind(TodoListComponent);
    bind(TodoDetailComponent);
    // Initialize routes.
    bind(RouteInitializerFn, toValue: moduleRouteInitializer);
    // Turn on listening to Window.onHashChange event.
```

```
bind(NgRoutingUsePushState,
    toValue: new NgRoutingUsePushState.value(false));
  }
}
```

In this case, route paths are paths after the hash sign in your URL. That's, for example, index.html#/add or index.html#/detail/3. However, you could tell AngularDart to match the entire URL and not just the hash part by setting the following:

```
bind(NgRoutingUsePushState,
    toValue: new NgRoutingUsePushState.value(true));
```

But this isn't very common.

Routes can be also nested:

```
'detail': ngRoute(
    path: '/detail/:taskId',
    mount: {
      'edit': ngRoute(
          path: '/edit',
          view: 'view/edit.html'),
    }
)
```

This would match routes such as /detail/3/edit, but we're not going to use it here in order to keep the example simple.

Model

Instead of keeping tasks as a list of strings like we did in the preceding section, we'll turn it into a class called Task:

```
// lib/service/task.dart
class Task {
  int id;
  String title;
  String when;

  Task(this.id, this.title, this.when);
}
```

This is pretty simple, just three public properties and a constructor. We'll see that we can print object properties straight into the template.

Then, for practical reasons, we'll move default tasks into a JSON file in web/default_tasks.json:

```
[{"id":1,"title":"Buy more cat food","when":"12:00"},
{"id":2,"title":"Feed the cat","when":"11:00"},
{"id":3,"title":"Do the laundry","when":"17:15"}]
```

View

Now, create two HTML templates in the web/view directory. First, we'll create add.html:

```
<!-- web/view/add.html -->
<h2>Add a new task</h2>
<p>when: <input type="time" ng-model="newTask['when']"></p>
<p>title: <input type="text" ng-model="newTask['title']"></p>
<button type="button"
    ng-click="addTask(newTask['when'], newTask['title'])">Add
</button>
```

Now, let's move on to creating detail.html:

```
<!-- web/view/detail.html -->
<h2>detail</h2>
<todo-detail all-tasks="tasks"></todo-detail>
<a href="#/add">add task</a>
```

These two HTML files represent templates for routes that a user can navigate to. The content of one of these templates will be inserted by Angular Dart into the <ng-view> tag according to the current matching route. We'll explain Angular directives used in these templates in a moment.

Component

Let's see the first part of our updated TodoListComponent class:

```
// lib/component/todo_list.dart
// Mark class as Component with an annotation.
@Component(
    selector: 'todo-list', // CSS selector for this component
    templateUrl: 'todo_list.html',
    exportExpressions: const ['newTaskParams', 'addTask']
)
class TodoListComponent {
  // Parameters for a new task.
  Map<String, dynamic> newTask = {};
  String title = "My Todo list";
  // Keep all my tasks in a list.
```

```
List<Task> tasks = [];
// Term for quick search among my tasks.
String search = '';

TodoListComponent() {
  // Load default tasks. We can't use async/await here because
  // class constructor can't return a Future object and
  // therefore can't be declared with async keyword.
  HttpRequest.getString('/default_tasks.json').then((response) {
    List<Map<String, String>> decoded = JSON.decode(response);

    decoded.forEach((Map<dynamic, String> taskData) {
      // Force integer value.
      int id = int.parse(data['id'].toString());
      // Append a new task to the list.
      tasks.add(new Task(id, data['title'], data['when']));
    });
  });
}
/* … */
}
```

You can see that we switched from `template` to `templateUrl`. As this template is going to be in the same directory as `todo_list.dart`, which isn't accessible by a browser, we need to tell AngularDart where to find it. Locate the following in `pubspec.yaml`:

```
transformers:
- angular
```

Replace the preceding lines with:

```
transformers:
- angular:
    html_files:
      - lib/component/todo_list.html
      - lib/component/todo_detail.html
```

Also, we used a new `exportExpressions` option. This tells AngularDart about expressions that aren't discoverable statically. This might be quite confusing at first sign. When you run an app using AngularDart, it automatically looks for expressions used in your code and generates a map of all getters in the `main_static_expressions.dart` file. This file is imported right at the top of `main.dart` when you publish your application with **Pub Build** (or run it in Dartium from Dart Editor).

We use both the `addTask()` method and the `newTaskParams` public property, but inside the `add.html` template, which is loaded dynamically and is therefore not found by AngularDart when generating `main_static_expressions.dart`. If you forgot to set expressions manually with `exportExpressions`, Dart will throw an error:

```
Missing getter: (o) => o.myLostProperty
```

You'll probably see this type of error a few times when using AngularDart, so if you're not sure whether all the getters that you use are found statically, you can take a look at `main_static_expressions.dart` and check what it found for you.

```
Sources  Content scripts  Snippets          main.dart    main_static_expressions.dart ×
▶ ○ (no domain)                            1  library Chapter_07_angulardart_todo_list_extended.web.main.generated_expressions;
▶ ○ file://                                2
▼ ○ localhost:8080                         3  import 'package:angular/change_detection/change_detection.dart';
  ▶ □ packages                             4
    index.html                             5  final Map<String, FieldGetter> getters = {
    main.dart                              6    r"newTaskParams": (o) => o.newTaskParams,
    main_generated_type_factory_maps.dar   7    r"addTask": (o) => o.addTask,
    main_static_expressions.dart           8    r"select": (o) => o.select,
    main_static_metadata.dart              9    r"urls": (o) => o.urls,
    main_static_type_to_uri_mapper.dart   10    r"value": (o) => o.value,
                                          11    r"bind": (o) => o.bind,
                                          12    r"valueExpression": (o) => o.valueExpression,
                                          13    r"onAbort": (o) => o.onAbort,
                                          14    r"onBeforeCopy": (o) => o.onBeforeCopy,
                                          15    r"onBeforeCut": (o) => o.onBeforeCut,
```

We see that the first two expressions are those that we defined in `exportExpressions`.

Next, we loaded the default tasks in the constructor and filled the `tasks` list with instances of the `Task` class.

Finishing TodoListComponent

Now we can finish `TodoListComponent` with methods to add and remove tasks:

```dart
class TodoListComponent {
  /* ... */

  void addTask(DateTime when, String title) {
    // Convert DateTime to HH:mm format.
    String str = "${when.hour.toString().padLeft(2, '0')}:"
              + "${when.minute.toString().padLeft(2, '0')}";

    // Find max id among all current tasks.
    int maxId = tasks.length == 0
        ? 1 : tasks.map((elm) => elm.id).toList().reduce(max);

    // Create a new instance of Task and append it to the list.
```

```
      tasks.add(new Task(maxId + 1, title, str));

      newTask = {};
    }

    // Remove task by id.
    void removeTask(MouseEvent e, int id) {
      e.preventDefault();
      tasks.removeWhere((task) => task.id == id);
    }
  }
```

We can already see how we create new tasks with two inputs and a button in `add`. `html`. Let's recap the input fields and buttons here with emphasized `ng-*` directives:

```
<input type="time" ng-model="newTask['when']">
<input type="text" ng-model="newTask['title']">
<button type="button"
    ng-click="addTask(newTask['when'], newTask['title'])">
Add</button>
```

Every change in inputs is propagated to the `newTask` map (that's the `ng-model` directive). Note that `newTask` is an empty map at the beginning.

Then, when you click on the button, we call the `addTask()` method and pass both arguments right from the template. The `addTask()` method creates a new task and sets `newTask = {}` at the end, which clears both inputs (two-way data binding).

Now, we'll create the template for our `TodoListComponent` in `todo_list.html`:

```
<!-- lib/component/todo_list.html -->
<h1>{{ title }}</h1>
<ng-view></ng-view>
<h2>My tasks</h2>
Search: <input type="search" ng-model="search">

<ul>
<li ng-repeat="t in tasks|filter:{'title':search}|orderBy:'when'">
  {{ t.when }} - <a href="#/detail/{{ t.id }}">{{ t.title }}</a>
  <a href="" ng-click="removeTask($event, t.id)">[remove]</a>
</li>
</ul>
<p ng-if="tasks.length == 0">Congratulations!</p>
```

We already mentioned that the template for the current matching route is placed in `<ng-view>`. On a page load, it's going to be `add.html` because it's marked as default. We tied only a small part of the application to routes, but you can change the entire layout with `<ng-view>` as well.

The `ng-repeat` directive is extended with two formatters. A **formatter** is basically a function that takes input data, processes it, and returns it. In Angular templates, formatters can be chained with the | character, and always take the result of the expression on their left-hand side as the input.

Our example uses two formatters:

- `filter`: This passes only items that match the defined criteria. You can use just a simple expression and the `filter` formatter will check all items' properties and if any of them contain the searched term, it will be passed to the output (for example, `filter:'the'`). We can also tell the `filter` to search in just one property by passing a map as an argument (in our example, we're searching only in task titles). The input list remains unchanged.

- `orderBy`: This sorts the input list by a property. The input list remains unchanged.

The `ng-repeat` directive creates a new scope for each clone, which means that each `<li>` tag has its own instance of `t` representing a task.

Note that we set the `href` attribute of `<a>` to #/detail/id. Changing the URL's hash doesn't load a new page but it's fetched by AngularDart's router, and the route that matches this URL is evaluated (for us, the content of `<ng-view>` is replaced by an appropriate template).

The `ng-click="removeTask($event, t.id)"` directive is the same as `addTask()` but uses a special `$event` variable provided automatically by AngularDart. We need to use it because by default, `<a>` changes a browser's location to what's in the `href` attribute. But that's not what we want, so we call `preventDefault()` on the event to prevent the default browser behavior (that's the first line of the `removeTask()` method).

At the end of `todo_list.html`, we have another `ng-if` directive, which causes itself and its subtree to be visible only when the expression is evaluated to `true`. There are actually two methods for showing/hiding elements in Angular:

- `ng-if`: When the expression is evaluated as `false`, it removes the entire subtree from the DOM. When it's `true`, it has to create the entire tree again. This directive also creates a new scope.

- `ng-show`: When the expression is evaluated as `false`, the DOM subtree is just hidden but still exists in the DOM. This directive doesn't create a new scope.

In many cases, these two are interchangeable. Just if you know you don't need new scopes, or the subtree is relatively small and is showed/hidden many times during the page's lifetime, it's probably better to use ng-show.

The last thing is the task's detail, which is a component declared in todo_detail.dart. We already saw in detail.html where it's going to be placed:

```
// lib/component/todo_detail.dart
// Usage: <todo-detail all-tasks="tasks"></todo-detail>
@Component(
    selector: 'todo-detail', // CSS selector for this component.
    templateUrl: 'todo_detail.html'
)
class TodoDetailComponent {
  // One way data binding, this component needs a reference
  // to all tasks but won't modify it internally.
  // Note that this property has to be public.
  @NgOneWay('all-tasks')
  List<Task> allTasks = null;

  // Task id from route parameters.
  int _id;

  Task _task = null;

  // Constructor that takes route parameters.
  TodoDetailComponent(RouteProvider routeProvider) {
    _id = int.parse(routeProvider.parameters['taskId']);
  }

  // Custom getter to avoid unnecessary iterations of the list.
  Task get task {
    // We need to check if allTasks isn't null.
    if (_task == null && allTasks != null) {
      allTasks.forEach((Task t) {
        if (t.id == _id) _task = t;
      });
    }
    return _task;
  }
}
```

This component is instantiated by AngularDart every time the URL matches the route with the detail.html template because it contains the <todo-detail> element.

We annotated the List<Task> allTasks property with @NgOneWay('all-tasks'), which tells AngularDart to put the result of an expression in the element's all-tasks attribute into the allTasks property. With this, we connected TodoListComponent and TodoDetailComponent components together.

Data bindings

There are three different annotations to bind attributes to object properties:

- NgOneWay: This is one way-data binding. The expression result from the attribute is passed to the object. Any change in the expression variable reevaluates the entire expression and a new value is passed to the object's property. However, changing the object's property doesn't propagate back to the expression's variable. Therefore, this is one-way (or unidirectional) binding.

  Note that when passing entire objects, AngularDart doesn't make copies of them. It passes just their references, so changing its properties actually changes the original object. For example, if we set _task.title = "hello" in the **task** getter, it would change its title in TodoListComponent as well. But setting allTasks = [] will just create a new list and assign its reference to the allTasks property. The original reference passed from the attribute's expression remains unchanged.

- NgTwoWay: This is two-way data binding. Changing the property value will be propagated back to the attribute's variable. Also, changing the attribute variable will change the value of the tied property.

- NgAttr: This is another unidirectional connection similar to NgOneWay but the attribute's values is passed as is, although you can use interpolation with "mustaches" {{ }}.

The difference between `NgOneWay` and `NgAttr` is that if we used `NgAttr` in `TodoDetailComponent`, AngularDart would take the attribute's "tasks" value as a string and wouldn't evaluate it as an expression. Therefore, this would throw an error because we can't assign a string to a variable of type `List`.

As `TodoDetailComponent` is instantiated every time we create the `<todo-detail>` element, we can define a constructor that accepts a `RouteProvider` object with all route parameters. For our purpose, this is the task's ID.

We can't rely on the order of variable bindings, and it's possible that the `task` getter in `TodoDetailComponent` will be called before the `allTasks` property is set. For this reason, we need to check whether `allTasks` was already set inside the `task` getter before we try to iterate it.

The last template is `todo_detail.html`, which is very simple:

```
<ul>
  <li>id: {{ task.id }}</li>
  <li>when: {{ task.when }}</li>
  <li>title: {{ task.title }}</li>
</ul>
```

The directory structure with all the files should look like this.

Finally, we can run our application in the browser.

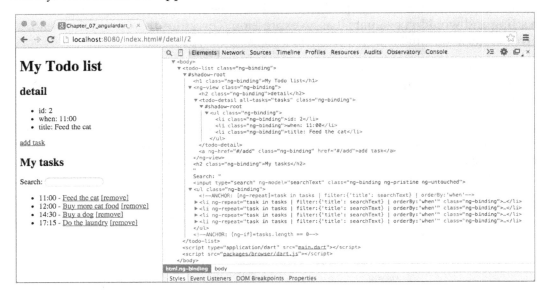

You can try that any change is immediately propagated to the view and things such as filtering the task list by the title (writing into the search input field) work and we didn't have to even touch the DOM by ourselves.

Don't worry if all this seems complicated to you, especially if you've never used any Angular before. We encourage you to download the source code for this example and play with it or take a look at the official tutorials at `https://angulardart.org/tutorial/`.

A book component in AngularDart

We already saw how to encapsulate a 3D book from *Chapter 4*, *Developing a Mobile App with Dart*, into a polymer.dart custom element. Now we'll do the same but in AngularDart now.

We can skip `main.dart`, because there's nothing new for us there, and see `<body>` in `index.html`:

```
<!-- web/index.html -->
<body>
  <p>angular: <input type="number" ng-model="elementsCount"></p>
  <shelf books-count="elementsCount"></shelf>

  <script type="application/dart" src="main.dart"></script>
</body>
```

Note that we're setting `ng-model` outside any component, so it'll be kept in the root scope, which is automatically set to `<html>`. Also, we're using `<input type="number">`, which tells AngularDart to convert the input from this field into an integer automatically.

The `<shelf>` element has one custom attribute called `books-count`, and we'll also use `cssUrl` to set a custom CSS file for this Shadow DOM:

```
// lib/component/shelf.dart
@Component(
    selector: 'shelf',
    templateUrl: 'shelf.html',
    cssUrl: 'shelf.css'
)
class ShelfComponent {
  @NgOneWay('books-count')
  int booksCount;
}
```

The `shelf.html` HMTL template is following:

```
<!-- lib/component/shelf.html -->
<h2>AngularDart</h2>
<div>
  <angular-book
      ng-repeat="book in booksCount | intToList"
      cover-image="{{ $even ? 'cover-old.jpg' : 'cover-new.jpg'}}"
      base-color="{{ $even ? '#000' : '#da944c'}}">
  </angular-book>
</div>
```

This time, we're using a custom formatter in the `ng-repeat` directive because `ng-repeat` can iterate only collections but `booksCount` is an integer that we'll use to create a `List` object with this number of items. Each iteration of `ng-repeat` creates a few local properties that might be useful:

- `$index`: This is the index (offset) of a current item (0 … n – 1)
- `$even`: This is true if this item is at an even index
- `$odd`: This is true if this item is at an odd index
- `$first`: This is true if this item is the first in the collection
- `$last`: This is true if this item is the last in the collection
- `$middle`: This is true if this item is neither the first nor the last item in the collection

The code for our custom formatter goes to `int_to_list.dart`:

```
// lib/formatter/int_to_list.dart
@Formatter(name: 'intToList')
class IntToListFormatter {
  List call(dynamic num) {
    int intValue;
    // Make sure the value is an integer.
    if (num is String) intValue = int.parse(num);
    intValue = (num == null ? 0 : num);

    return new List.filled(intValue, true);
  }
}
```

Just don't forget to include `int_to_list.dart` as a dependency among components in `main.dart`:

```
// web/main.dart
MyAppModule() {
  /* … */
  bind(IntToListFormatter);
}
```

The code for `book` elements is very simple as well. Note that we're not going to encapsulate them in the Shadow DOM because we already created one in `ShelfComponent` and we don't need another one:

```
// lib/component/book.dart
@Component(
    selector: 'angular-book',
    templateUrl: 'book.html',
    cssUrl: 'book.css',
    useShadowDom: false
)
class BookComponent {
  @NgAttr('cover-image')
  String coverImage;

  @NgAttr('base-color')
  String baseColor;
}
```

In the template, we can use the `<angular-book>` element itself as a wrapper for all the book's faces. The rest looks very similar to the template in the polymer.dart example:

```
<!-- lib/component/book.html -->
<div class="front" style="background-image: url(./{{coverImage}})">
</div>
<div class="left" style="background-color: {{baseColor}}"></div>
<div class="right"></div>
<div class="back" style="background-color: {{baseColor}}"></div>
<div class="top"></div>
<div class="bottom"></div>
```

We don't even need to include CSS files here, because it's basically what we already used in polymer.dart. Feel free to download the source code for this chapter if you have any hesitations or go back to the previous chapter.

Just remember that the `:host` CSS selector can be used to refer to the current custom element in both polymer.dart and AngularDart.

Finally, this is our result in the browser:

We wrapped both books in just one Shadow DOM. In polymer.dart, all elements have their Shadow DOM unless you extend the default `PolymerElement` class, copy children elements directly to the `host` element, and therefore, bypass the Shadow DOM. Frankly, this isn't recommended because it violates the main purpose of Polymer, but you might run into a situation where you really want to avoid using the Shadow DOM (like `core-list` for example). With AngularDart, this is made very simple by just setting one property.

By quickly comparing the same functionality implemented in polymer.dart and AngularDart, we can see that the one written in AngularDart is actually shorter.

AngularDart can, with a little effort, connect various parts of a web application together. It's intended to be a self-contained framework that solves logic, model, and presentation aspects of applications.

Polymer.dart is best for creating independent and reusable components that can be imported into any web page, regardless of the rest of the code.

What is Angular 2.0?

AngularJS and AngularDart are two separate projects in two different languages, sharing the same philosophy. This requires two of Google's developer teams to maintain two codebases. Angular 2.0 is still in development and its release date is unknown, yet there are some fundamental concepts known already.

Angular 2.0 is developed in AtScript, which is a language created by Google that extends Microsoft's TypeScript. TypeScript itself is a superset of JavaScript and should be partly compatible with the ECMAScript 6 standard in the future. Right now, it has to be compiled to JavaScript as well.

That said, there will be just one codebase for Angular 2.0 in AtScript, which can be compiled into JavaScript or Dart.

Why is Angular 2.0 not written in Dart?

That's an obvious question. Angular 2.0 has to be easy to use for both Dart and JavaScript developers, and here's the problem with Dart. Dart doesn't compile into code that is easily reusable in JavaScript. In *Chapter 1*, *Getting Started with Dart*, and *Chapter 2*, *Practical Dart*, we already talked about how the Dart team is canceling efforts to implement the Dart VM into Chrome, and they're focusing on improving the `dart2js` compiler instead (or maybe switching to a completely new compiler `https://github.com/dart-lang/dev_compiler`), which is a logical step in this situation.

Performance tips for AngularDart

In most use cases, AngularDart will run fast enough for you to not even notice that there is a framework under the hood. However, when dealing with large DOM trees such as tables or long lists (let's say thousands of DOM elements), you can get hit by Angular very hard.

The basic ideas behind optimization is that we want to reduce the number of expressions that Angular watches and try to keep the scope hierarchy shallow. Internally, Angular uses the so-called **digest loop**, which is executed every time a value in the model changes. It has to check all watched expressions and see whether they've changed, and if they did, it has to propagate the change further until there are no pending changes.

When we talked about scopes, we mentioned that some Angular directives create new scopes and when used inappropriately, they might have significant performance impact. That's why we'll take a look at some performance optimization tips that reduce the number of watched expressions, together with a few recommendations on what you shouldn't do in order to speed up you application.

You can check out which directives create new scopes in the documentation at `https://docs.angulardart.org`.

Avoiding nesting ng-repeat directives

It might seem logical to display a table like this:

```
<table>
  <tr ng-repeat="row in rows">
    <td ng-repeat="col in columns">{{ row.columns[col.id] }}</td>
  </tr>
</table>
```

This is an absolute overkill for Angular. With 100 rows and five columns, this makes 500 scopes. If you added just a single `ng-if` directive inside `<td>`, it would be 1,000 scopes because each `ng-if` creates a new scope too.

Instead, try to preprocess your templates. Of course, you have to use `ng-repeat` to actually print each row, but you can modify the template to use just one `ng-repeat` directive:

```
<table>
  <tr ng-repeat="row in rows">
    <td>{{ row.columns[1] }}</td>
    <td>{{ row.columns[2] }}</td>
    <td>{{ row.columns[3] }}</td>
  </td>
</tr>
```

For very large lists, you can also use Polymer's `<core-list>` element that we saw in the previous chapter.

Using track by for ng-repeat

In the to-do list example, we used a filter to sort tasks by their time. A big disadvantage of this approach is that every time you change the sorting order or add/remove a task, Angular has to remove the entire DOM subtree and create it again.

This is why you can use a special track by keyword, which tells ng-repeat how to uniquely identify each row and therefore, when you manipulate the iterated collection, it can check whether the row was already created. So, a better and recommended way to use ng-repeat in the to-do list would be:

```
<li ng-repeat="t in tasks|filter:term|orderBy:p track by t.id">
```

Avoiding excess formatter usage

Another common performance bottleneck that isn't obvious is the excessive use of formatters, usually in loops. For example, let's say we have a formatter called niceDate that turns a timestamp into a date according to the user's locale:

```
<li ng-repeat="time in collection">{{ time|niceDate }}</li>
```

Firstly, Angular doesn't know that the formatter won't modify the original variable. This is the same problem that we already saw with NgOneWay, as described earlier. Your formatter might change an object's property and Angular has to process it in a digest cycle. This is why Angular actually runs formatters twice.

Concretely, you change an object's property in your model and Angular evaluates an expression with your formatter. But you might change an object's property again in the formatter and Angular has to be sure it caught all the changes that occurred, and therefore, it has to evaluate formatters again.

Secondly, this formatter doesn't even need to be used in the expression. You can format the date somewhere in your code and just print the formatted date.

Not everything needs to be in Angular

When using Angular, things work like magic. Although you shouldn't modify the DOM tree that is already maintained by Angular, you still can change CSS styles or classes (again, those that aren't already managed by Angular; otherwise, it might lead to unpredictable behavior) by yourself.

For example, if you wanted to display a list with 1,000 items and then filter (show/hide) them in some manner, you can use this code:

```
<ul>
    <li ng-repeat="item in collection track by item.id"
        ng-show="showMe(item)">{{ … }}</li>
</ul>
```

We don't want to use a formatter to filter out unwanted items, because it would have to iterate the entire collection and the `ng-show` directives will still create 1,000 expressions for Angular to watch.

Instead, we can just drop the `ng-show` directive and show/hide the `<li>` tags by directly changing their styles by setting, for example, `display: none` right in your code.

Note that this will make the code a little harder to understand for people who aren't familiar with what your application does, but remember that this is also an option. In even more extreme cases, you can write parts of your application in JavaScript outside Dart and move the root scope from the default `<html>` tag with `ng-app`.

Just don't think that when you start using Angular, absolutely everything has to be managed via Angular.

Summary

This chapter was quite extensive. We encourage you to try AngularDart by yourself and see that it's actually not as difficult as it might seem. The benefits are really big, and at the end of the day, they will save you a lot of time developing the same things over and over again, and let you focus on your application's logic instead.

The next chapter is going to be about writting CLI apps and server-side scripts in Dart.

7
Server-side Applications with Dart

In this chapter, we'll take a look at developing command-line server-side apps. In particular, we'll learn the following topics:

- How to process command-line arguments with the `args` package
- Writing a small chat app with a WebSockets server in Dart
- How to access filesystem with the `dart:io` library
- Storing data to the MySQL database with the `sqljocky` package
- Writing a small web server using the `route` package
- How to use Apache and nginx servers as reverse proxies for Dart HTTP servers

This chapter assumes that you already have at least basic experience with CLI scripts or Unix environments in general. If you're a Windows user, take a look at Cygwin (`www.cygwin.com`), which is a Unix-like environment for Windows, or ideally, install Ubuntu into a virtual machine. The Dart SDK is now available for Debian and Ubuntu Linux distributions, while Dart Editor is currently available only for Ubuntu Linux.

We'll set off with a few notes about Dart VM and then go to processing command-line arguments, because that's what you'll probably use every time you start developing a CLI app.

The standalone Dart VM

The Dart SDK comes with a standalone Dart VM to run command-line apps such as `pub` or `dart2js`. You can find it in `<dart-sdk-dir>/bin/dart`. It accepts command-line arguments such as `-h` for help or `-c` to enable the checked mode. There are also special options for the Observatory tool (we'll use it in *Chapter 8, Testing and Profiling the Dart Code*). These aren't very interesting for us now, but feel free to check out `https://www.dartlang.org/tools/dart-vm/` for a complete list of all supported options.

The standalone Dart VM is mostly the same environment as the VM implemented in the Dartium browser. The entry point for an app is a top-level `main()` function, but this time, it accepts a list of arguments passed from the command line:

```
main(List<String> args) {
  /* ... */
}
```

With the standalone Dart VM, you can't use libraries specific to the browser environment, such as `dart:html`, of course. On the other hand, you can use `dart:io` to access the filesystem or create subprocesses, listen to signals, and so on. We're going to use this package a lot in this chapter.

Parsing CLI arguments with the args package

As we're going to write a WebSockets server, we might want to control it with some options passed from the command line, for example, a port number where the WebSockets server is listening or a command to stop the server when running in the background.

Let's create a new project with the `Console Application` template, add the `args` package to its dependencies, and start writing the WebSockets sever by defining its CLI options.

We'll create an instance of `ArgParser` and define possible options with the `addOption()` and `addFlag()` methods. Flags are options that can only have `true`/`false` values:

```
// bin/server.dart
import 'package:args/args.dart';
import 'dart:io';
```

```
main(List<String> args) async {
  ArgParser parser = new ArgParser();

  // This is probably self-explanatory.
  parser
    ..addOption('port', abbr: 'p', defaultsTo: '8888')
    ..addOption('pid-file', defaultsTo: 'var/websockets.pid',
        help: 'Path for a file with process ID')
    ..addOption('cmd', abbr: 'c', defaultsTo: 'start',
        allowed: ['start', 'stop'],)
    ..addFlag('help', abbr: 'h', negatable: false);

  var argResults = parser.parse(args);

  if (argResults['help']) {
    print(parser.usage);
  } else if (argResults['cmd'] == 'stop') {
    // Stop server by sending a SIGTERM signal.
  } else {
    // Start the WebSockets server.
  }
}
```

For example, an option definition with the following code allows us to use the CLI arguments `--port 1234`, `--port=1234`, `-p 1234` or `-p1234`:

```
parser.addOption('port', abbr: 'p')
```

As a flag, we have:

```
parser.addFlag('help', abbr: 'h', negatable: false);
```

In our case, `-h` or `--help` mean `true` and omitting the flag is `false`. This format of arguments is often called "GNUism".

The actual processing of CLI arguments happens in the `ArgParser.parse()` method, which returns a map-like object with parsed values. Note that we don't necessarily need to use arguments passed from the CLI and we can process a custom list of strings.

A big advantage of `ArgParser` is that it can automatically generate usage help for you in the `ArgParser.usage` property. If you run our app with the `--help` or `-h` argument, it dumps all possible options and flags with their defaults, descriptions, and allowed values:

```
$ dart bin/server.dart --help
-p, --port              (defaults to "8888")
    --pid-file          Path for a file with process ID
                        (defaults to "var/websockets.pid")


-c, --cmd               [start (default), stop]
-h, --help
```

We don't need to worry about the `-c` option right now and start writing the WebSockets server first.

Apart from options and flags, the `args` package also supports creating commands similarly to `git commit` or `apt-get install`. However, `args` gets quite confusing with commands, so I would recommend that you try the `unscripted` package (`https://pub.dartlang.org/packages/unscripted`) instead, because it lets you map commands directly to class methods and make the configuration more readable.

Writing a chat app with the WebSockets server

WebSockets is a protocol for bidirectional communication between a web browser and a server. The fact that a server can actively send you messages is the most important thing and is probably the only reason why you might want to use WebSockets in the future. There used to be some fallbacks for browsers that don't support WebSockets, such as long pooling, but we're not going to use any of them and assume that our browsers are up to date with proper WebSockets support.

Our chat WebSockets server spawns an HTTP server that listens to WebSockets headers and implements a handshake between the two endpoints to switch to the WebSockets protocol (the so-called **upgrade request**).

Later, we'll log all chat messages in a MySQL database.

So first, we'll create an HTTP server that implements "upgrade requests" and a class that holds all our active WebSockets connections. All we need to write HTTP servers is part of the dart:async package:

```
// bin/server.dart
import 'package:args/args.dart';
import 'dart:io';
import 'dart:async';
import 'dart:convert';
import 'dart:collection';

// Class representing a client connected to the chat server.
class WebSocketsClient {
  String name;
  WebSocket ws;

  WebSocketsClient(this.ws);
  Future close() => ws.close();
}

class ChatWebSocketsServer {
  // Hold all connected clients in this list.
  List<WebSocketsClient> _clients = [];

  // Add a new client based on his WebSocket connection.
  void handleWebSocket(WebSocket ws) {
    WebSocketsClient client = new WebSocketsClient(ws);
    _clients.add(client);
    print('Client connected');

    // In a real app we would probably wrap JSON.decode() with
    // try & catch to filter out malformed inputs.
    // Stream.map() returns a new Stream and processes each item
    // with callback function. In our case it decodes all JSONs.
    // onDone is called when the connection is closed by client.
    ws.map((string) => JSON.decode(string))
      .listen((Map json) {
        handleMessage(client, json);
    }, onDone: () => close(client));
  }
```

```dart
    // Handle incoming messages.
    void handleMessage(WebSocketsClient client, Map json) {
      /* ... */
    }
    // Client closed their connection.
    void close(WebSocketsClient client) { /* ... */ }
  }

  main(List<String> args) {
    // Args parser configuration as above.
    HttpServer httpServer;

    if (argResults['help']) { /* ... */
    } else if (argResults['cmd'] == 'stop') { /* ... */
    } else if (argResults['cmd'] == 'start') {
      ChatWebSocketsServer wsServer = new ChatWebSocketsServer();

      print('My PID: $pid');
      int port = int.parse(argResults['port']);
      print('Starting WebSocket server');

      var address = InternetAddress.LOOPBACK_IP_V4;
      HttpServer httpServer = await HttpServer.bind(address, port);
      StreamController sc = new StreamController();
      sc.stream.transform(new WebSocketTransformer())
          .listen((WebSocket ws) {
            wsServer.handleWebSocket(ws);
      });

      // Listen to HTTP requests.
      httpServer.listen((HttpRequest request) {
        // You can also handle different URL with request.uri.
        // if (request.uri == '/ws') { }
        sc.add(request);
      });
    }
  }
```

This is our app in a nutshell. We use `StreamController` and `WebSocketTransformer` classes to upgrade the client's HTTP request to the WebSockets connection.

What's interesting here is the `handleWebSocket()` method. Notice in particular how we're using closures with the `client` variable. Both `handleMessage()` and `close()` are in a closure and have their own reference to `client`, so even with multiple calls to `handleWebSocket()`, we can still easily identify which client invoked each event.

The `handleMessage()` method is the core of the entire server app and it's called for every incoming message from all clients. Our app will handle three types of messages:

- The client changing their chat name
- Posting a message that is broadcasted to all connected clients
- Requesting the entire available chat history

We can finish the server part with all we need for now:

```dart
// bin/server.dart
// A single item in the chat history.
class ChatMessage {
  String name;
  String text;

  ChatMessage(this.name, this.text);
  String get json => JSON.encode({'name': name, 'text': text});
}

class ChatWebSocketsServer {
  List<WebSocketsClient> _clients = [];
  // Chat history.
  ListQueue<ChatMessage> _chat;
  static const int maxHistory  = 100;

  ChatWebSocketsServer() {
    _chat = new ListQueue<ChatMessage>();
  }

  void handleWebSocket(WebSocket ws) { /* same as above */ }

  // Handle incoming messages.
  void handleMessage(WebSocketsClient client, Map json) {
    if (json['type'] == 'change_name') {
      client.name = json['name'];
```

```
      } else if (json['type'] == 'post' && client.name.isNotEmpty) {
        ChatMessage record =
            new ChatMessage(client.name, json['text']);
        // Keep only last maxHistory messages.
        _chat.addLast(record);
        if (_chat.length > maxHistory) _chat.removeFirst();
        broadcast(record);

      } else if (json['type'] == 'init') {
        // Send chat history to the client.
        // Let's not bother with performance for simplicity reasons.
        _chat.forEach((ChatMessage m) => client.ws.add(m.json));
      }
    }
  }

  // Client closed their connection.
  void close(WebSocketsClient client) {
    print('Client disconnected');
    // Remove the reference from the list of clients.
    client.close().then((_) =>
        _clients.removeAt(_indexByWebSocket(client.ws)));
  }

  // Close connection to all clients.
  // This is used only on server shutdown.
  Future closeAll() {
    // Make a list of all Future objects returned by close().
    List<Future> futures = [];
    _clients.forEach((client) => futures.add(client.ws.close()));
    // ... and wait until all of them complete.

    return Future.wait(futures);
  }

  // Send a message to all connected clients.
  void broadcast(ChatMessage message) {
    // Method add() sends a string to the client.
    _clients.forEach((client) => client.ws.add(message.json));
  }
```

```
  // Get index for this connection from the list of clients.
  int _indexByWebSocket(WebSocket ws) {
    for (int i = 0; i < _clients.length; i++) {
      if (_clients[i].ws == ws) return i;
    }
    return null;
  }
}
```

We're using `ListQueue<T>` here to store chat messages because it has the `removeFirst()` and `addFirst()` methods with constant time complexity.

Although the code is quite long, it's not hard to understand. Note the `broadcast()` method that sends a message to all connected clients because we have the `WebSocket` connections for all of them. When a client disconnects, we call its `close()` method and remove it from the list of clients.

Client-side WebSockets

The HTML and Dart code for a web browser using WebSocket is simple as well:

```html
<!-- web/index.html -->
<body>
  <p>Name: <input type="text" id="name"></p>
  <div id="chat"></div>
  <p>Message: <input type="text" id="msg">
    <button id="btn-send">Send</button></p>
  <script type="application/dart" src="main.dart"></script>
</body>
```

There are just two input fields and a button:

```dart
// web/main.dart
import 'dart:html';
import 'dart:convert';

main() {
  WebSocket ws = new WebSocket('ws://127.0.0.1:8888');

  ws.onOpen.listen((e) {
    print('Connected');
    ws.sendString(JSON.encode({'type': 'init'}));
  });
```

```
    // Automatically decode all incoming messages.
    ws.onMessage.map((MessageEvent e) =>
      JSON.decode(e.data)).listen((Map j) {
        var a = '<p><b>${j['name']}</b>:
${j['text']}</p>';
        querySelector('#chat').appendHtml(s);
    });

    querySelector('#name').onKeyUp.listen((e) {
      ws.sendString(JSON.encode({
        'type': 'change_name',
        'name': e.target.value
      }));
    });

    querySelector('#btn-send').onClick.listen((e) {
      InputElement input = querySelector('#msg');
      ws.sendString(JSON.encode(
          { 'type': 'post', 'text': input.value }));
      input.value = '';
    });
  }
```

Both server and browser are using the WebSocket class, but they aren't the same. The browser's WebSocket comes from the dart:html package, while the WebSocket used in the server is from dart:io. This is why we're sending data with both sendString() and add() methods.

The WebSocket class in the browser has a couple of streams. The most interesting are onOpen and onMessage. We used onOpen to request the entire chat history from the server. Then, onMessage decoded all the data sent from the server and because we're expecting just chat messages, we appended a simple HTML to the main container.

To test the server, we can run it without any parameters:

```
$ dart bin/server.dart
My PID: 15725
Starting WebSocket server
```

Then, open multiple tabs, with `index.html`, and try to set different names and write a few messages. The messages should immediately appear in all tabs. In Developer Tools, we can also see both sent and received messages from the server via WebSockets:

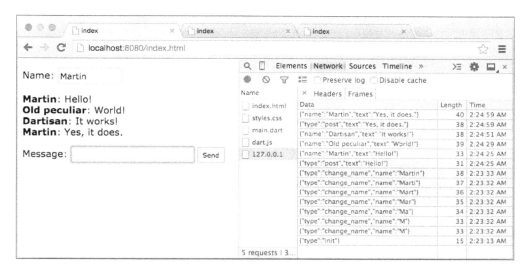

Listening to Unix signals and basic I/O operations

If we wanted to run this server in a real-life application, we would ideally run it in the background, disassociate from the terminal with no output, and so on. We can do this with the `nohup` utility that prevents a process from terminating, even when the parent process terminates by ignoring the `SIGHUP` signal. Note that this isn't the same as running a daemon process. Daemons have to follow a predefined behavior, such as closing all file descriptors, changing the current directory, redirecting output, and more.

Before we do this, we need to be able to stop the server when it's running in the background. We could use `ps | grep server.dart`, but there could be more processes with this name running at the same time and we may not know which one is the one we want to terminate.

Running the server as a background process

We should create a well-behaved process that listens to termination signals, such as SIGTERM and SIGINT, to properly close all WebSocket connections and the HTTP server.

For this reason, we'll save our server's **process ID (PID)** into a file on launch and listen to the two signals. Then, running dart bin/server.dart -c stop will read the PID and use Process.kill() to send a signal to the currently running server process:

```
main(List<String> args) async {
  /* the rest is unchanged */
  } else if (argResults['cmd'] == 'stop') {
    // stop process by sending a SIGTERM signal
    String pidFile = argResults['pid-file'];
    String pid = await (new File(pidFile).readAsString());
    Process.killPid(int.parse(pid), ProcessSignal.SIGTERM);
  } else if (argResults['cmd'] == 'start') {
    /* Create HTTP server and so on... */
    // Save process PID to a file.
    String path = argResults['pid-file'];
    File file = await (new File(path)).create(recursive: true);
    await file.writeAsString(pid.toString());

    void shutdown(ProcessSignal signal) {
      print('Received signal $signal');
      // Remove the file with PID.
      pool.close();

      // At this point it's better not to use await because
      // we can call all tasks asynchronously and just wait until
      // all of them are finished.
      await Future.wait([
        new File(argResults['pid-file']).delete(),
        httpServer.close(),
        wsServer.closeAll(),
      ]);
```

```
    // End this process now with code 0.
    exit(0);
}

ProcessSignal.SIGTERM.watch().listen(shutdown);
ProcessSignal.SIGINT.watch().listen(shutdown);
}
}
```

We used the `File` class to create both a new file and a directory with `create(recursive: true)`. Both `File` and `Directory` classes are based heavily on `Future` objects. However, some methods have synchronous and asynchronous implementations (for example, there are `delete()` and `deleteSync()` methods).

To stop the server, we run `server.dart` again, which sends a signal to the PID of the process that's currently running the server.

Now, we can run `server.dart` again:

```
$ nohup dart bin/server.dart > /dev/null 2>&1 &
```

Using `> /dev/null` redirects all `stdout` to `/dev/null` (discarding all output), `2>&1` redirects `stderr` to `stdout`, and finally, `&` runs the process in the background.

We don't even care what a server's PID is because it's saved in a file and is automatically read and killed with:

```
$ dart bin/server.dart -c stop
```

The server process gently closes all connections and terminates.

Enumerated types

Dart 1.9 brought another new keyword called `enum` to define a **fixed set of values**. In our example from the preceding section, we could define fixed number of commands as:

```
enum Command { start, stop }
```

Later in the code, we could check which command we want to use without comparing strings, as we did in the preceding example, but rather compare `Command` enums like this:

```
cmd = Command.start;
if (cmd == Command.stop) { /* ... */ }
```

We can update our `main()` method and convert a string `argResults['cmd']` command into a `Command` enum value:

```
Command cmd = Command.values.firstWhere((Command c) {
  String cmdString = c.toString().split('.')[1].toLowerCase();
  return cmdString == argResults['cmd'].toLowerCase();
});

// Then follow with ifs to handle each command.
if (cmd == Command.stop) {
  // ...
} else if (cmd == Command.start) {
  // ...
}
```

The `Command.values` property is a constant that contains a `List` object with all possible values for this enum. Calling `c.toString()` returns a string representation of an enum's value which in our case are `Command.start` and `Command.stop`. The `List.firstWhere()` method iterates all items in the list until the first one that returns a Boolean `true` value.

Typedefs

Everything in Dart is an object; including functions that can be passed as arguments. However this approach has one caveat. If we define a variable to hold, for example a callback function called when a user posts a new message, we could do:

```
class ChatWebSocketsServer {
  var newMsgCallback;
  /* ... */
  void handleMessage(WebSocketsClient client, Map json) {
    /* ... */
    if (newMsgCallback != null) {
      newMsgCallback(record.name, record.text);
    }
  }
}

main(List<String> args) async {
  /* ... */
  wsServer.newMsgCallback = (String from, String msg) {
    print("$from: $msg");
  };
}
```

This is all right as far as we know that the callback function takes two `String` parameters. What could happen is that we might accidentally try to use a callback function that takes a different number or different types of parameters in both `ChatWebSocketsServer` class or `main()`.

By defining `var newMsgCallback`, we lost track of the function definition. We could actually assign it any variable. That's why Dart has **typedefs** which is like a function definition prefixed with `typedef` keyword and without any body:

```
typedef void MessageCallback(String from, String msg);

class ChatWebSocketsServer {
  MessageCallback newMsgCallback;
  /* ... */
}
```

The `newMsgCallback` property has to have the same definition as `MessageCallback` typedef. Dart's type check can now warn you if you try to assign it anything else.

Using MySQL as a storage

As we want to store all chat messages in a MySQL database for further investigation, we'll add a dependency with a MySQL connector called `sqljocky`. Right now, it can only connect to MySQL via TCP; using Unix sockets doesn't work, so make sure you don't have the `skip-networking` option enabled in the MySQL configuration (it disables all TCP connections completely).

We'll keep it very simple and use just one table with three columns in a database called `dart_chat`. You can create the table structure with this SQL query:

```
CREATE TABLE 'chat_log' (
  'id' int(11) unsigned NOT NULL AUTO_INCREMENT,
  'name' varchar(255) NOT NULL DEFAULT '',
  'text' text NOT NULL,
  'created' datetime NOT NULL,
  PRIMARY KEY ('id')
) ENGINE=InnoDB DEFAULT CHARSET=utf8;
```

In Dart, we'll connect to MySQL and pass the connection to `ChatWebSocketsServer`:

```
import 'package:sqljocky/sqljocky.dart';
main() {
  /* same as above */
  } else if (argResults['cmd'] == 'start') {
```

```
        ConnectionPool pool = new ConnectionPool(host: '127.0.0.1',
          port: 3306, user: 'root', password: null, db: 'dart_chat');
        wsServer = new ChatWebSocketsServer(pool);
        /* same as above */
    }
}
```

Then we will update the `ChatWebSocketsServer` class:

```
ChatWebSocketsServer {
  /* ... */
  Query _preparedInsertQuery;

  ChatWebSocketsServer(ConnectionPool pool) {
    _chat = new ListQueue<ChatMessage>();

    // The same like calling new Future(() {});
    (() async {
      // Preload chat history asynchronously.
      String selectSql = """
          SELECT * FROM chat_log ORDER BY created DESC LIMIT 0,100
      """;
      var results = await pool.query(selectSql);
      results.forEach((Row row) {
        var msg = new ChatMessage(
            row.name.toString(), row.text.toString());
        _chat.addFirst(msg);
      }

      String insertSql = """
      INSERT INTO chat_log (name,text,created) VALUES (?,?,NOW())""";
      _preparedInsertQuery = await pool.prepare(insertSql);
    })();
  }
  /* the rest remains unchanged */
}
```

In the constructor, we made one query that matches the 100 latest chat records and prepopulates the chat history. Then, we used `pool.prepare()` to create a so-called prepared query, which serves as a template that we can reuse multiple times by just executing it with a list of parameters.

> You should never insert variables directly into SQL queries and always use prepared queries to avoid SQL injection attacks (http://en.wikipedia.org/wiki/SQL_injection).

The last thing is to execute a prepared statement when a client sends a new message:

```
void handleMessage(WebSocketsClient client, Map json) {
  /* same as above */
  } else if (json['type'] == 'post' && client.name.isNotEmpty) {
    /* same as above */
    _preparedInsertQuery.execute([record.name, record.text]);
  } else if (json['type'] == 'init') { /* ... */ }
}
```

We don't even have to work with the database connection outside the constructor of `ChatWebSocketsServer`. The `_preparedInsertQuery.execute()` method makes an asynchronous call but we don't need to wait until it finishes and broadcast the message to all clients in the meantime. A few persisted records might look like this:

Apart from what we used here, `sqljocky` can also run a prepared query multiple times in one call with `Query.executeMulti()`. In our case, it could be:

```
Query.executeMulti([['name1', 'text1'], ['n2', 't2'], [...]]);
```

This actually runs a single query for each list. Sometimes it's better to run multiple queries in a single transaction for performance reasons:

```
var trans = await pool.startTransaction();
await trans.query('...');
await trans.query('...');
await trans.query('...');
await trans.commit();
```

Basically, every operation with the database is asynchronous, so we'll use the `await` keyword a lot (just imagine how awful this would be with nested callbacks).

Finally, when we're done with using the database, we should close it with `pool.close()`, which, in contrast to the most close methods, doesn't return a `Future` object.

We're using just MySQL here, but you can find connectors to probably all common database engines available today at `https://pub.dartlang.org`. It's worth noting that this connector is relatively new and its functionality is very simple. It's incomparably more primitive than projects such as SQLAlchemy for Python or Doctrine 2 for PHP.

Writing an HTTP server with the route package

We've already seen that creating an HTTP server isn't hard. We could handle different URLs with a few `if` statements:

```
var addr = InternetAddress.LOOPBACK_IP_V4;
var server = await HttpServer.bind(addr, port);
server.listen((HttpRequest request) {
  if (request.uri == '/contact') {
    // …
  } else if (request.uri == '/blog') {
    // …
  }
});
```

This would work and would be enough for very simple usage. However, you usually need to specify URIs with parameters and also serve static content. We can use the `route` package, which is an interesting package that works on both client and server sides. We'll use it here on the server side.

So, create a new project and add two dependencies: `route` and `http_server`. The second package contains the `VirtualDirectory` class that we'll use to make an entire directory available for URIs that don't match any route. Also, create a directory called `public` in the project's root, where we'll put all static content:

```
// bin/server.dart
import 'dart:io';
import 'package:route/server.dart';
```

```dart
import 'package:http_server/http_server.dart';
// Define patterns for all possible URLs.
final homeUrl = new UrlPattern('/');
final articleUrl = new UrlPattern('/article/(.+)');

main() async {
  // Get this script's path.
  var static = Platform.script.resolve('../public').toFilePath();

  var addr = InternetAddress.LOOPBACK_IP_V4;
  var server = await HttpServer.bind(addr, 8081)
  print('Server running ...');
  // Add route handlers.
  // We're using [Stream.map()] to log all requests.
  var router = new Router(server.map(debugHandler))
    ..serve(homeUrl, method: 'GET').listen(showHome)
    ..serve(articleUrl, method: 'GET').listen(showArticle);

  // Serve entire directory.
  var virDir = new VirtualDirectory(staticDir);
  // Show contents of directories, rather disable it in production.
  virDir.allowDirectoryListing = true;
  // Disable following symbolic links outside the server root dir.
  virDir.jailRoot = true;
  // Use this handler for all URLs that don't match any route.
  virDir.serve(router.defaultStream);
}

HttpRequest debugHandler(HttpRequest request) {
  // We'll just log the requested URI, but at this place you could
  // also check user's credentials from cookies and so on.
  print(request.uri);
  return request;
}
void showHome(HttpRequest request) {
  request.response.write("Hello, I'm your new homepage!");
  // Send response.
  request.response.close();
}

void showArticle(HttpRequest request) {
  // Get URI parameter.
  String slug = articleUrl.parse(request.uri.path)[0];

  request.response.write('You requested article "$slug"');
  /* Do whatever you want here */
  request.response.close();
}
```

Now we have an HTTP server that handles two specific URI patterns and serves the entire content of the `public` directory. The `Router()` constructor accepts a `Stream` object, but we want to log all requests to the server, so we used the `map()` method that converts each value of the stream into a new value and returns a new `Stream` object. As we don't want to modify requests in any way, we just return them in `debugHandler()`.

Note that route handlers don't need to return anything. We're writing its response (including return codes and headers) right into the `request.response` object.

I placed a few test files in my `public` directory:

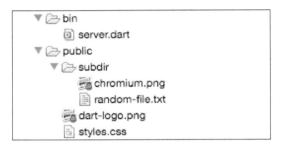

Now, run the server and test a few URLs in a browser:

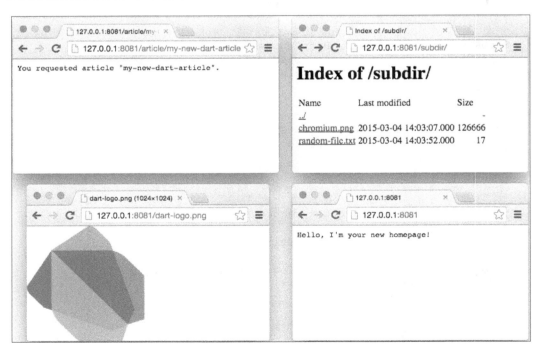

In the console, I can see the requested URIs:

```
$ dart bin/server.dart
Server running ...
/dart-logo.png
/
/article/my-new-dart-article
/subdir/
```

An obvious question is whether this is useful in a real-world application. Well, you probably wouldn't serve static files with the Dart server and use a better optimized server such as nginx instead, because it's well tested; supports caching, compression, usage statistics, and countless modules; and has already been in production for years all around the world.

Using Dart as a full-stack language

For dynamic content, we could use Dart's HTTP server, but we probably wouldn't expose it directly to the Internet and rather put in behind a reverse proxy.

If you really wanted to expose your server to anyone, you need to tell the HTTP server to accept connections from all IPs with ANY_IP_V4 instead of LOOPBACK_IP_V4:

```
var addr = InternetAddress.ANY_IP_V4
```

This also applies to WebSockets servers.

Accessing Dart servers via Apache or nginx reverse proxies lets you stay with LOOPBACK_IP_V4 (127.0.0.1, aka localhost), which is generally safer.

Using Apache as a proxy for the Dart HTTP server

As we said, we can use Apache to serve all static content and proxy all nonstatic requests to the Dart HTTP server. You can modify your hosts file to point dart.localhost to 127.0.0.1 if you're already using virtual hosts on your computer and add a new directive to the Apache configuration:

```
<VirtualHost *:80>
  DocumentRoot "/project/path/Chapter_07_route_http_server/public"
  ServerName dart.localhost
```

```
RewriteEngine on
RewriteCond %{DOCUMENT_ROOT}/%{REQUEST_FILENAME} !-f
RewriteRule ^/(.*)$ http://127.0.0.1:8081/$1 [P,QSA,L]

<Directory "/project/path/Chapter_07_route_http_server/public">
  Order allow,deny
  Allow from all
</Directory>
</VirtualHost>
```

If you've ever used PHP with Apache, you've probably already met `.htaccess` files to pass all nonstatic requests to `index.php`. These rewrite rules use exactly the same principle. They check whether a requested URI is an existing file with `RewriteCond %{REQUEST_FILENAME} !-f` and if it is not, they pass the request to `http://127.0.0.1:8081/<request-uri>`, where our Dart HTTP server is running. The response is automatically sent back to the client.

The `[P]` flag at the end is crucial because it activates Apache's reverse proxy. Using this kind of reverse proxy in Apache requires `mod_proxy`, `mod_proxy_html`, and `mod_rewrite` modules installed.

We can test that it really works by looking at the Apache access log and comparing it with the Dart server's requests. For example, I see these logs in my `/var/log/apache/access_log` file:

```
127.0.0.1 [15:38:20] "GET /dart-logo.png HTTP/1.1" 200 21903
127.0.0.1 [15:38:24] "GET / HTTP/1.1" 200 29
127.0.0.1 [15:40:22] "GET /article/my-article HTTP/1.1" 200 40
127.0.0.1 [15:40:22] "GET /subdir/random-file.txt HTTP/1.1" 200 17
```

These are requests to the Apache server, which should pass two of them to the Dart server, and it did:

```
$ dart bin/server.dart
Server running ...
/
/article/my-article
```

Using nginx as a proxy for the Dart HTTP server

The same principle works for the nginx configuration:

```
location / {
    root "/project/path/Chapter_07_route_http_server/public";
    try_files $uri @darthttpserver;
}

location @darthttpserver {
    proxy_set_header X-Real-IP  $remote_addr;
    proxy_set_header Host $host;
    proxy_set_header X-Forwarded-For $proxy_add_x_forwarded_for;
    proxy_pass http://127.0.0.1:8081;
}
```

The `try_files` directive tests whether `$uri` exists as a file under the `root` directory, and if it doesn't, it makes an internal redirect to `@darthttpserver`, where we pass the request to the Dart HTTP server.

With nginx, we can be a little more generous and redefine HTTP headers sent to the Dart server with `proxy_set_header`. Here, we're setting headers such as client's real IP, because from Dart's point of view, it seems like all requests come from localhost.

Executing Dart as CGI and Apache mod_dart

Although it's possible to run the Dart code as a CGI script, it's not a good idea for real-world applications. It basically runs a standalone Dart VM for each request, which causes a new process to spawn, allocates memory, loads Dart libraries, compiles them, and runs your code. It causes significant overhead, which can be easily avoided by running Dart as an HTTP server.

There is also an Apache module called `mod_dart` that promised embedding Dart VM into Apache workers. The same approach is commonly used with Apache and `mod_php5`. Unfortunately, the project is currently not maintained any more. Rumors among Dartisans say that you can compile it with a few modifications but it's stale and possibly unstable with security holes and you should never use it.

If you have to use Apache, stay with reverse proxying requests as we saw earlier.

Summary

The goal of this chapter was to show you that you can start using Dart as a full-stack language right now. The most useful way might be as a single purpose WebSockets server, because you probably have some experience with server-side scripting in other languages already and switching to a different environment isn't easy. The decision might depend on more people than just you and support for the Dart language from server administrators probably isn't very common.

In the next chapter, we'll have a look at unit testing Dart code. We'll also make a few notes about the Observatory tool and two features of Dart that we haven't talked about yet; mixins and operator overloading.

8
Testing and Profiling the Dart Code

Testing is an essential part of any development process. There are many different approaches and libraries that can be used to test your applications, and we'll take a look at one of them.

In this chapter, we'll talk about:

- Unit testing in Dart, a very common way to test independent parts of applications that can range from single methods to entire classes
- Operator overloading and mixins, two more features of Dart
- A few notes about testing AngularDart apps
- A short introduction to Observatory, Dart's built-in profiler

In contrast to the previous chapters, we won't run our code in the browser but write console applications instead.

Testing strategies for web apps

It's hard to tell what is generally the best way to test web apps. There are quite a lot of tools already and probably apart from choosing the right tool, you'll need to think about what you should test, where, and how.

We'll mostly talk about unit testing because it can be used for both web and standalone apps. Then, in the context of AngularDart, we'll mention the so-called end-to-end tests with Karma and Protractor. We're not able to cover everything in this chapter, so if you want to know more about testing in JavaScript and in the browser, take a look at the master's thesis of Vojtěch Jína, a current employee of Google, who has been working on AngularJS for more than 3 years: `https://github.com/karma-runner/karma/raw/master/thesis.pdf`.

Unit testing

The motivation for writing unit tests shouldn't just be a simple way to test existing code, there are more benefits to consider:

- The fundamental idea behind unit tests is to write isolated testable code. To achieve this, it makes developers write smaller single-purpose methods and therefore avoid writing long spaghetti-like code.

- Refactoring existing code is easier because you can rewrite and test code in smaller portions. Refactored code should pass the same tests as the original code.

- Tests themselves can be considered as documentation and examples of expected behavior.

For this example, we'll write a console application that finds all numbers that are prime numbers, and all its digits are used only once. This is, for example, the number 941, because it's a prime number and contains each digit only once. On the other hand, the number 1,217 is a prime number but contains the digit 1 twice, so that's not what we're looking for.

Then, we'll extend our example with another method that returns a list of all prime numbers smaller that a certain maximum.

We'll start by creating a new Dart project and adding the unittest dependency. However, this time, we're not going to add it in the dependency directive but rather dev_dependencies. Both of these have the same meaning but the second one is pulled by the pub tool only when your package is not pulled as a third-party dependency. In other words, if you run pub get on this package, it will also download dev_dependencies, but if you use it as a dependency of another package, it won't be downloaded because it's not required by this package for regular usage. The dev_dependencies directive is useful mostly to specify packages that are necessary for developing or testing the package. Also, we can add another dependency called args, which is a library for parsing command-line arguments that we've already seen in the previous chapter, and we'll use it here later.

 If you're creating projects in Dart Editor, you can select the Console App template, and it adds the unittest dependency for you along with creating the basic directory structure.

First, we'll create a method that checks whether an integer is a prime number, but for testing purposes, we'll introduce a bug in it:

```dart
// lib/methods.dart
import 'dart:math';
import 'dart:convert';

bool isPrime(int num) {
  // Intentionally broken, number 2 is a prime.
  if (num <= 2) {
    return false;
  } else if (num % 2 == 0) {
    return false;
  }

  for (int i = 3; i < pow(num, 0.5).toInt() + 1; i += 2) {
    if (num % i == 0) return false;
  }

  return true;
}
```

Then, we write our test code that uses the `unittest` library and is runnable from the console:

```dart
// test/test_is_prime.dart
import 'package:unittest/unittest.dart';
import 'package:unittest/vm_config.dart';
import 'package:Chapter_08_unittest/methods.dart';

void main() {
  // Tell unit test library about our output format.
  useVMConfiguration();
  defineTests();
}

void defineTests() {
  test('3 is a prime', () {
    expect(isPrime(3), isTrue);
  });

  test('2 is a prime', () {
    expect(isPrime(2), isTrue);
  });
}
```

A test is defined by calling the `test()` function, which comes from the `unittest` library and defines a single test case. It takes two arguments, the name of the test, and an anonymous function that represents the test's content with one or more `expect()` calls.

Each `expect()` function takes actual and expected values as arguments, respectively. The expected value is a subclass of the `Matcher` class, which is responsible for resolving whether these two match.

In our case, we have a single `expect()` call that checks whether the value returned from `isPrime(3)` is equal to the Boolean `true` value. The `isTrue` instance is a constant defined in `unittest` package. As you might have guessed, there are quite a lot of predefined matchers.

The most commonly used matchers are `isMap`, `isList`, `isNull`, `isNotNull`, `isTrue`, `isFalse`, `isNaN`, and `isNotNaN` — which are pretty self-explanatory. The following table has more predefined matchers:

Matcher name	Description
`isEmpty`	Matches empty strings, maps, and collections using their `isEmpty` property.
`throws`	Tests whether a function or a returned `Future` object throws an exception.
`equals`	For iterables and maps, this tests all elements recursively. For anything else, this tests equality with `==`.
`completes`	Matches a `Future` object that completes the execution successfully.
`same`	Matches whether actual and expected values are the same object.
`isInstanceOf<T>`	Matches when the actual object is an instance of `<T>`.
`returnsNormally`	Tests whether the function doesn't throw any exception. This also suppresses all exceptions thrown.
`hasLength`	Matches when the object has the `length` property, and its value is equal to the expected value.
`contains`	For strings, this checks for a substring; for collections, this checks for a matching element; and for map objects, this checks for existing key.
`isIn`	Tests whether the actual value is among expected values. The expected value can be a string, collection or a map.
`equalsIgnoringCase`	Matches when values are equal when compared case-insensitively.
`orderedEquals`	Matches whether the collection has the same number of elements and whether they are in the same order.
`unorderedEquals`	Matches whether the collection has the same number of elements in any order. Note that this method has the worst case complexity O^2, which means that it can be very slow on a collection with larger number of elements.

There are also specialized matchers for integer ranges, particular exceptions, iterables, and maps, and you can define your own matchers as well. For a complete list of all existing matchers, refer to the API reference at http://www.dartdocs. org/documentation/matcher/0.12.0-alpha.0/index.html#matcher/matcher.

We can run our test from the console. The useVMConfiguration() function tells Dart unit testing library what output format we want and what exit status code to use. We know that our isPrime function has a bug, so we're expecting it to fail.

We could also run unit tests in a browser by including another configuration:

```
import 'package:unittest/html_config.dart';
```

After this, we would have to use useHtmlConfiguration() instead. Note that only one configuration can be used at a time.

```
● ● ●                          test — bash — 95×22
martin:test martin$ dart test_is_prime.dart
unittest-suite-wait-for-done
PASS: 3 is a prime

FAIL: 2 is a prime
  Expected: true
    Actual: <false>

  package:unittest/src/simple_configuration.dart 15:28   _ExpectFailureHandler.fail
  package:matcher/src/expect.dart 121:9                  DefaultFailureHandler.failMatch
  package:matcher/src/expect.dart 95:29                  expect
  test_is_prime.dart 19:11                               defineTests.<fn>
  dart:isolate                                           _RawReceivePortImpl._handleMessage


1 PASSED, 1 FAILED, 0 ERRORS
martin:test martin$ echo $?
1
martin:test martin$ 
```

You can safely ignore the first line, unittest-suite-wait-for-done, which is a message for the environment running these tests.

Then, we see that the first test passed but the second test failed because it returned a false Boolean while the expected value was true. Although the second test failed, it's not an error. In other words, the tested function ran correctly but didn't return the expected value.

With echo $?, which is a standard Unix command to return the status code for the previous command, we see that it returned 1 because one of the tests failed or threw an error. If all tests passed, the return code would be 0 (values 0 and 1 are standard for success and error states, respectively, in Unix-based systems).

We can simulate an error by, for example, changing the function definition to `isPrime(var num)` and then testing with `expect(isPrime('foo'), isTrue)`. Changing `int num` to `var num` bypassed the static type check and we might not even notice that the rest of `isPrime` expects its parameter to be an integer.

Running the tests this time throws an error instead of just failing the test:

```
● ● ●                          test — bash — 95×22
martin:test martin$ dart test_is_prime.dart
unittest-suite-wait-for-done
PASS: 3 is a prime

ERROR: 2 is a prime
  Test failed: Caught Class 'String' has no instance method '<='.

  NoSuchMethodError: method not found: '<='
  Receiver: "foo"
  Arguments: [2]
  dart:core                                  Object.noSuchMethod
  package:Chapter_08_unittest/methods.dart 7:11  isPrime
  test_is_prime.dart 19:19                   defineTests.<fn>
  dart:isolate                               _RawReceivePortImpl._handleMessage



1 PASSED, 0 FAILED, 1 ERRORS
martin:test martin$ echo $?
1
martin:test martin$
```

Let's fix the `isPrime()` function:

```
/* … */
bool isPrime(int num) {
  if (num < 2) {
    return false;
  } else if (num == 2) {
    return true;
  } else if (num % 2 == 0) {
    return false;
  }
  for (int i = 3; i < pow(num, 0.5).toInt() + 1; i += 2) {
    if (num % i == 0) return false;
  }
  return true;
}
```

The following screenshot shows the output of the fixed code:

```
● ◎ ●                    test — bash — 75×14
martin:test martin$ dart test_is_prime.dart
unittest-suite-wait-for-done
PASS: 3 is a prime

PASS: 2 is a prime


All 2 tests passed.
unittest-suite-success
martin:test martin$ echo $?
0
martin:test martin$
```

Finally, both tests passed and the return code is `0`.

The second function that we're going to write is called `hasUniqueDigits()`. It takes an integer as a parameter and returns `false` if any of the digits appear more than once:

```
// lib/methods.dart
import 'dart:convert';

bool hasUniqueDigits(int num) {
  String numAsStr = num.toString();
  Set<int> bytes = UTF8.encode(numAsStr).toSet();
  return bytes.length == numAsStr.length;
}
```

We convert the integer to a `String` object, then we convert it to `List<int>` with the `encode()` method, and then to `Set<int>`. A set can contain each value only once, so if the list contains two same digits, then the lengths of the set and the length of the string won't match.

The tests for this function are basically the same as the tests for `isPrime()`:

```
// test/has_unique_digits_test.dart
import 'package:Chapter_08_unittest/methods.dart';
import 'package:unittest/unittest.dart';
```

```
import 'package:unittest/vm_config.dart';

void main() {
  useVMConfiguration();
  defineTests();
}

void defineTests() {
  test("doesn't have unique digits", () {
    expect(hasUniqueDigits(123441), isFalse);
  });

  test('has unique digits', () {
    expect(hasUniqueDigits(42), isTrue);
  });
}
```

When we put everything together, we'll create a command-line application that takes two arguments:

- --max or -m followed by a number. This is the maximum number that we'll check with isPrime() and hasUniqueDigits(). By default, it's set to 100.

- --silent or -s, which is just true or false whether it's set or not. When true, print only the largest found number; otherwise, print all of them.

The args library that we added as a dependency earlier will do all the parsing for us:

```
// bin/unique_and_prime.dart
import 'package:args/args.dart';
import 'package:Chapter_08_unittest/methods.dart';

void main(List<String> args) {
  final parser = new ArgParser();
  parser.addOption('max', abbr: 'm', defaultsTo: '100');
  parser.addFlag('silent', abbr: 's');
  ArgResults argResults = parser.parse(args);
  int max = int.parse(argResults['max']);
  bool silent = argResults['silent'];

  int maxNum = 0;
  for (int i = 1; i < max; i += 2) {
    if (isPrime(i) && hasUniqueDigits(i)) {
      maxNum = i;
      // Print all found numbers only when silent isn't true.
```

```
        if (!silent) print("$i");
      }
    }

    // When silent is set, print the max found number.
    if (silent) {
      print("$maxNum");
    }
  }
```

We can run this application by issuing the following command:

$ dart unique_and_prime.dart

This command uses default values for --silence and --max and prints each number on a new line.

$ dart unique_and_prime.dart --silent -m 1000000

With this command, we check the first million integers (actually, we increment by 2, so that's just half of them), and if we consider that we check for primes in another loop, that's quite a lot of operations. To measure processing time, we can prepend the console command with time and see that it actually runs reasonably fast:

```
● ● ●                    bin — bash — 75×12
martin:bin martin$ time dart unique_and_prime.dart --silent -m 1000000
987631

real    0m0.325s
user    0m0.310s
sys     0m0.017s
martin:bin martin$
```

We can add one more function to lib/methods.dart. Let's say we want to use our isPrime() function to generate a list of first *n* primes in the same order in which they were found:

```
List<int> getPrimes(int total) {
  List<int> found = new List<int>();
  int num = 1;
  while (found.length != total) {
    if (isPrime(num)) {
```

```
        found.add(num);
      }
      num++;
    }
    return found;
  }
```

To check the correct results, we can use the `orderedEquals` matcher:

```
void main() {
  useVMConfiguration();
  defineTests();
}

void defineTests() {
  test('first 10 primes', () {
    var actual = getPrimes(10);
    List<int> expected = [2, 3, 5, 7, 11, 13, 17, 19, 23, 29];
    expect(actual, isList);
    // This test is redundant, orderedEquals() checks it for us.
    // expect(actual, hasLength(10));
    expect(actual, orderedEquals(expected));
  });
}
```

Asynchronous tests

If we wanted to test code that's called asynchronously, such as Ajax, filesystem operations, or basically all IndexedDB functions, we need to use the `expectAsync()` function instead of `expect()`. The reason is that `unittest` doesn't know that we're not interested in the actual function call that makes an asynchronous call but are rather interested in its callback. Therefore, this example won't do what we want:

```
// test/test_async.dart
void defineTests() {
  // This is wrong, don't do this.
  test('test async', () {
    int actual;
    new Timer(new Duration(milliseconds:1000), () {
      print('callback fired!');
      actual = 42;
    });
```

```
    expect(actual, equals(42));
  });
}
```

Then, when we run this test, it returns immediately and reports a failed test with:

```
FAIL: test async
  Expected: <42>
    Actual: <null>
```

Instantiating a `Timer` class schedules a callback to be called 1 second in the future, but `unittest` doesn't know about it, and it thinks that this is all you wanted to do.

In order to fix this, we'll wrap the `Timer` class's callback with the `expectAsync()` call and pass the original callback to it:

```
test('test async callback', () {
  new Timer(new Duration(seconds:1), expectAsync(() {
    print('callback fired!');
    int actual = 42;
    expect(actual, equals(42));
  }));
});
```

When we run the test again, it works as we wanted:

```
$ dart test_async.dart
callback fired!
PASS: test async
All 1 tests passed.
```

The `expectAsync()` function can take optional `count` and `max` parameters that will make the test pass only if you call its callback an exact number of times or the maximum number of times, respectively.

Note that tests can make use of the `async` and `await` keywords from Dart 1.9 just like any other Dart app.

Test groups

Usually, it makes sense to group tests into logic blocks. This means putting tests that check the same or similar functionality together to make the output more readable and easily trackable in case it goes wrong. Groups can be also nested.

When using groups, we can make use of two more functions: `setUp()` and `tearDown()`. These are used to prepare local variables, such as instantiating objects or loading fixture data, and are called before and after each test (note that tests shouldn't rely on a state created by other tests). The `setUp()` and `tearDown()` methods can be nested just like groups and are called from the outermost to innermost for `setUp()` and the other way around for `tearDown()`. We can try to make our `test_is_prime.dart` file a little more complicated:

```
void defineTests() {
  group('True expected:', () {
    setUp(() => print('Outer setUp'));
    tearDown(() => print('Outer tearDown'));

    group('Lower bound:', () {
      setUp(() => print('Inner setUp'));
      tearDown(() => print('Inner tearDown'));
      test('3 is a prime', () {
        print('3 is a prime test content');
        expect(isPrime(3), isTrue);
      });
      test('2 is a prime', () {
        print('2 is a prime test content');
        expect(isPrime(2), isTrue);
      });
    });

    test('12197 is a prime', () =>
        expect(isPrime(12197), equals(isTrue)));
  });

  group('False expected:', () {
    test('21 is not a prime', () => expect(isPrime(21), isFalse));
    test('21357 is not a prime', () =>
        expect(isPrime(21357), equals(false)));
  });
}
```

See the order of `setUp()` and `tearDown()` functions. The first `setUp()` function is called for the outer group, then the inner, and after that, it calls the test itself. For `tearDown()` functions, the first group called is the inner and then the outer. The same procedure is applied for each test in the group:

```
$ dart test_is_prime.dart
Outer setUp
```

```
Inner setUp

3 is a prime test content

Inner tearDown

Outer tearDown

Outer setUp

Inner setUp

2 is a prime test content

Inner tearDown

Outer tearDown

Outer setUp

Outer tearDown

PASS: True expected: Lower bound: 3 is a prime

PASS: True expected: Lower bound: 2 is a prime

PASS: True expected: 12197 is a prime

PASS: False expected: 21 is not a prime

PASS: False expected: 21357 is not a prime
```

Note the order of outer/inner setUp()/tearDown() functions.

Running all tests

Every test that we defined in the test/test_*.dart files has its own main()
function that calls its defineTests() function, but calling each test by ourselves
isn't very practical, so we'll create an all.dart Dart script that imports all tests
and runs them at once:

```
// test/all.dart
import 'package:unittest/vm_config.dart';
import 'test_is_prime.dart' as test_is_prime;
import 'test_has_unique_digits.dart' as test_has_unique_digits;
import 'test_get_primes.dart' as test_get_primes;
import 'test_async.dart' as test_async;

void main() {
  useVMConfiguration();
  test_is_prime.defineTests();
  test_has_unique_digits.defineTests();
  test_get_primes.defineTests();
  test_async.defineTests();
}
```

At the end, running all tests is easy:

```
$ dart all.dart
```

Note that tests are called in the order in which they are defined.

Operator overloading and mixins

We'll take a look at two more Dart features that are useful in some situations but aren't crucial when using Dart, and you'll probably not use them on a daily basis.

Operator overloading

Dart lets us overload its default behavior when using standard operators such as ==, +, -, [], or [] =. A typical use case is when using 2D/3D vectors:

```
class Vector {
  int x, y;
  Vector(this.x, this.y);

  operator ==(Vector v) => this.x == v.x && this.y == v.y;
  operator  +(Vector v) => new Vector(this.x + v.x, this.y + v.y);
  operator  -(Vector v) => new Vector(this.x - v.x, this.y - v.y);
}
```

We can use unit testing to check whether operators work as expected:

```
var v1 = new Vector(5, 3);
var v2 = new Vector(7, 2);

Vector v3 = v1 + v2;
expect(v3.x, 12);
expect(v3.y, 5);

expect((v1 - v2) == new Vector(-2, 1), isTrue);

var v6 = new Vector(3, 5);
expect(v1 == v6, isFalse);
```

Unlike JavaScript, there's no === operator (three equal signs) in Dart that compares variables for having the same type and value. The way Dart actually compares objects is up to you by overloading their == operator. To check whether two object reference the same instance, you can use the top-level identity() function.

As another use case, we could extend the book shelf example from previous chapters with overloaded "array subscription" operators, [] and []=:

```
class Shelf {
  Map<String, Book> books = {};

  add(Book book) => books[book.title] = book;
  operator []=(String key, Book book) => books[key] = book;
  operator [](Book book) => books[book.title];
}

class Book {
  String title;
  Book(this.title);
}
```

This lets us use Shelf objects just like maps, where Book instances are stored with their names as keys:

```
var shelf = new Shelf();
var b1 = new Book('Book 1');
var b2 = new Book('Book 2');

shelf.add(b1);
shelf[b2.title] = b2;
expect(shelf[b1], same(b1));
```

Well, we could just call shelf.books[b2.title] = b2, but you get the idea how []= operator works.

There are quite a lot of operators to overload and we only used the most common ones here, but take a look at all of them at https://www.dartlang.org/docs/dart-up-and-running/ch02.html#overridable-operators.

Mixins

In *Chapter 1, Getting Started with Dart*, we mentioned that Dart has a single inheritance model with mixins. The proper definition of mixins is rather complicated (refer to the official definition for Dart at https://www.dartlang.org/articles/mixins/) but simply put, a mixin is a common behavior/feature shared among multiple unrelated classes. In practice, this means a set of methods and properties that are common to all classes implementing this mixin.

We can extend our book shelf example once more by adding a mixin, defining that each book and shelf can be described by keywords that can be arranged into genres:

```
class Genre {
  List<String> keywords = [];

  guessGenre() {
    // Try to guess what's the overall genre for this object.
    // Implementation is not interesting for us here.
  }
}
class Shelf extends Object with Genre {
  /* Remains unchanged. */
}

class Book extends Object with Genre {
  /* Remains unchanged. */
}
```

Mixins are implemented by the `with` keyword. Each class implementing mixins has to specify its parent class even when it's the default `Object` class. Both `Shelf` and `Book` classes now have the `keywords` property and a `guessGenre()` method.

The `Genre` mixin is just a class that has to follow three requirements:

- No constructors defined
- The super class is the default `Object` class
- No calls to the parent class with `super`

We can test both classes whether they properly implement the `Genre` mixin. Note that one class can implement multiple mixins at the same time:

```
// Objects created as above.
expect(shelf, new isInstanceOf<Genre>());
expect(b1, new isInstanceOf<Genre>());

expect(shelf.keywords, new isInstanceOf<List>());
expect(b1.keywords, new isInstanceOf<List>());

expect(shelf.guessGenre, new isInstanceOf<Function>());
expect(b1.guessGenre, new isInstanceOf<Function>());
```

When any of these tests fail, the code throws an exception, so outside unit tests, we could check whether an object implements a mixin rather with the `is` keyword:

```
if (shelf is Genre) {
  // Object shelf of class Shelf implements Genre mixin.
}
```

Testing AngularDart apps

If you're familiar with AngularJS, you've probably already seen the toolchain used to test AngularJS apps. For AngularDart, the toolchain will probably be very similar. Although AngularDart has reached a stable version already, there's not much to offer right now, but we can just take a look at what the future might look like. There are three main tools used in the Angular world:

- **Unit tests**: Just like what we're doing in this chapter, we can use unit tests to test some parts of Angular apps.

- **Karma**: This is a universal tool that takes your source code and test code and runs them in a browser for you. It's actually a web server that communicates with all browsers that you connect to. It can also automatically watch for changes in your source code and run tests without you running the tests by yourself. Karma isn't an AngularJS-specific tool, but it's used by its developers as well. There's a plugin for Dart already at `https://github.com/karma-runner/karma-dart`.

- **Protractor**: It's specifically designed to work with AngularJS. It uses WebDriverJS, which basically lets you run a browser without any graphical interface in CLI, where you can run tests. It can also emulate user inputs such as key presses or mouse clicks and even file uploads. Protractor "understands" AngularJS and lets you do things such as selecting elements by their Angular bindings or specific directives.

  There's an extension of Protractor for Dart apps but it's in a very early stage of development, so this is probably the biggest problem with testing AngularDart apps right now (this was also mentioned by the AngularDart developer James Deboer at *ng-conf 2014* at `https://www.youtube.com/watch?v=RqKUTGB-CxA`).

Automatic testing AngularDart without better tools is tedious when you have no control over Angular's digest cycle, and you'll probably end up calling `new Timer()` a lot to let Angular update its internal state and then test what you need, which is far from ideal.

Profiling with the Observatory tool

The Dart SDK comes with a profiling tool since version 1.4. It's still in development, so we're going to look at just the basic things. Observatory has a comfortable browser GUI that makes it easy to use for everyone. You're probably not going to spend much time profiling your apps unless you're working with large amounts of data or in a field where performance matters a lot (such as games). However, it's good to know that there's such tool and it's built right inside Dart's VM.

You can run the profiler for both the standalone Dart VM and web apps, but we'll take a look only at the standalone Dart VM, because we can easily run it from Dart Editor.

For this example, we'll reuse the fuzzy search code from *Chapter 2, Practical Dart,* and create a test CLI app that runs a few search queries:

```
import 'dart:io';
import 'dart:convert';
import '../../Chapter_02_doc_search/lib/FuzzySearch.dart';

main() {
  FuzzySearch fuzzy;

  void testSearch() {
    List testTerms = ['strpl','myslcom','imsz','png2w','arrdf'];
    testTerms.forEach((String term) {
      List results = fuzzy.search(term);
    });

    print(testTerms); // PLACE A BREAKPOINT HERE
  }

  // Load json file with our dictionary.
  var f = new File('../../Chapter_02_doc_search/web/dict.json');
  f.readAsString().then((text) {
```

```
    Map<String, dynamic> dict = JSON.decode(text);
    fuzzy = new FuzzySearch(dict.keys.toList());
    testSearch();
  });
}
```

This code runs our fuzzy search algorithm for five test terms. We're not interested in what it returns; we'll just use this code to see the Observatory profiler. Of course, we can profile apps on the run (like the WebSocket server that we made in the previous chapter), but it's probably more common to analyze just a small part of your app or maybe a single algorithm. Note that Observatory is part of the Dart VM and therefore, if you want to access it in the browser, the Dart VM has to be running. You can't run the profiler and analyze results later (which is the most common usage of profilers in languages such as PHP or Python).

Place a breakpoint at line 14 to make the Dart VM pause there. Now, run the app and watch the console window in Dart Editor. You should see something like this:

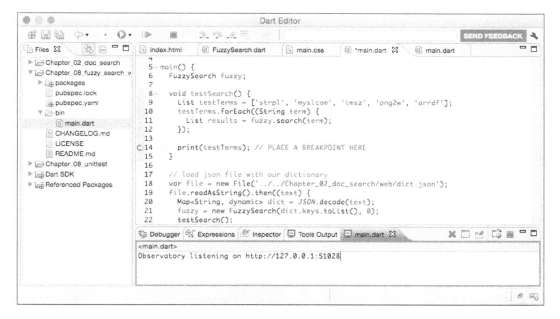

It says that the Observatory is running on port `51028`. The port number is not fixed, so you'll probably have a different one. Open this URL in a browser, and you'll see the GUI (it can be any browser, not just Dartium):

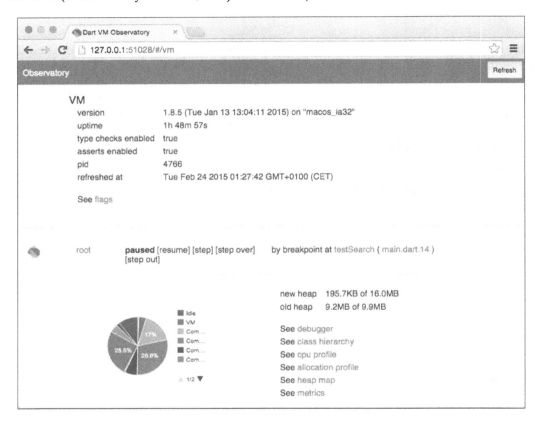

This is a lot of information; don't worry if you don't understand what it means. Just out of curiosity, click on **cpu profile** in the bottom-right list. Then, select **User** in **Tag Order** select box, and try to find out how much time our `FuzzySearch.search()` method took. It'll probably be very little—about 3 percent of the total VM's running time.

This was just a sneak peak of what Observatory is, and as we said previously, it's not stable yet and it'll change in the future. As you can see, the information that our method took 3 percent isn't very helpful because we would like to know what exactly took the most time in order to optimize it, so this is probably one of those things where Observatory will improve in newer versions.

One of the already useful features of Observatory is code coverage, which you can access from the main screen by clicking the filename. You can see code coverage for each file used by the Dart VM.

```
15      // Iterate entire list.
        List<String> result = list.where((String key) {
17        int ti = 0; // term index
18        // int si = 0; // key index
19        // Check order of characters in the search term and in the string.
          for (int si = 0; si < key.length; si++) {
            if (term[ti] == key[si]) {
              ti++;
              if (ti == term.length) {
24              return true;
25            }
26          }
27        }
28        return false;
        }).toList(growable: false);
30
31      // Custom sort function.
32      // We want the shortest terms to be first because it's more likely
33      // that what you're looking for is there.
        result.sort((String a, String b) {
          if (a.length > b.length) {
36          return 1;
          } else if (a.length == b.length) {
38          return 0;
39        }
```

All the line numbers in the green background were already executed until now.

Summary

Unit testing is a very useful method even if you're not trying to follow test-driven development rules. It helps you think about your code as single-purpose isolated components that can be tested independently when you're either developing or refactoring the code.

It's good to keep in mind that unit tests aren't able to catch every bug in the code. Their usefulness depends on scenarios that you can think of, and therefore, you can miss some hardly predictable situations. Unit tests usually don't test the integration of components and the performance of your code. There are also situations that you can't simulate, such as unexpected operation system behavior caused by other processes.

Try to remember that there's a profiler called Observatory right in Dart's VM, and you can easily use it for your needs.

9
Writing Native Extensions for the Standalone Dart VM

This is the last chapter. We'll look at a slightly more advanced topic, which is writing native extensions in C/C++ for the standalone Dart VM. Don't worry if you've never seen C or C++; we'll use a very intuitive approach while trying to stay practical. In this chapter, we'll work on two examples:

- Writing a fuzzy search algorithm as a C++ class and comparing its performance with the implementation shown in *Chapter 2, Practical Dart*

- Writing bindings for the exiv2 library to read EXIF image metadata

The main purpose of this chapter is to give you the whole picture of Dart as a language. Most of the time, you probably won't write native extensions even when using Dart as a server-side language. In this chapter, we want to show you the enormous and nearly unlimited potential of Dart.

The structure of native extensions

All native extensions in Dart are compiled as shared (also called dynamic) libraries and have to implement two main functions:

- The <extension_name>_Init() function that is called by the Dart VM when the extension is loaded. Most importantly, it registers a handler that returns references to the extension's functions (typically called ResolveName()). We can use it to initialize some local variables, but most of the time, you'll use the default function from the example given by the Dart team. We'll use the default one here as well.

- The ResolveName() function is called when we use the native keyword in Dart and is used to map functions from native extensions to Dart functions.

Typically, there's also a Dart class that wraps all calls to the native extension.

It's worth noting that there are conventions and caveats we have to follow. Otherwise, Dart won't be able to load our extension with quite an ambiguous error message: `library handler failed`. The premises are as follows:

- The filename must be prefixed with `lib`. For example, when importing a native extension called `hello_extension`, Dart is looking for a `libhello_extension.dll` file (`.so` for Unix-based systems or `.dylib` for OS X).
- Mind your Dart VM's build architecture. Even on 64-bit systems, it's very likely that you're running a 32-bit Dart VM that requires all native extensions to be built as 32-bit binaries. This implies that all libraries linked by your extension have to be compiled as 32-bit libraries. Of course, we can use universal libraries that contain both 32-bit and 64-bit builds.
- The `<extension_name>_Init()` function has to be defined even if you're not using it. For example, for the `hello_extension` extension, it has to be called `hello_extension_Init()`. Mind the capital "I".

For a more in-depth description about the compilation process and how to set up IDEs for various systems, refer to the official guide at `https://www.dartlang.org/articles/native-extensions-for-standalone-dart-vm`.

There are two types of extensions: **synchronous**, which run on Dart's main thread, and **asynchronous**, which don't block the main thread and communicate with Dart via ports. In this chapter, we'll use only synchronous extensions because they use a more intuitive approach and basically don't require any Dart code.

Writing a minimal native extension

We'll start by writing a very simple extension with just one function that takes Dart's `String` object as an argument and returns another `String` object with characters in a reverse order. Let's start by defining the two mandatory C functions, as we mentioned earlier.

The implementation here is based on the official example from `https://github.com/dart-lang/bleeding_edge/blob/master/dart/samples/sample_extension/sample_extension.cc`:

```
// Header files are part of Dart SDK.
#include "include/dart_native_api.h"
#include "include/dart_api.h"
```

```
Dart_NativeFunction ResolveName(Dart_Handle name,
                                int argc,
                                bool* auto_setup_scope) {

DART_EXPORT Dart_Handle fuzzy_search_Init(
        Dart_Handle parent_library) {
    if (Dart_IsError(parent_library)) {
        return parent_library;
    }
    // Register handler that is called every
    // time Dart's "native" keyword is used.
    Dart_Handle result_code = Dart_SetNativeResolver(
        parent_library, ResolveName, NULL);
    if (Dart_IsError(result_code)) {
        return result_code;
    }
    return Dart_Null();
}
// Raise a Dart exception if Dart_Handle contains an error value.
Dart_Handle HandleError(Dart_Handle handle) {
    if (Dart_IsError(handle)) {
        Dart_PropagateError(handle);
    }
    return handle;
}

void Hello(Dart_NativeArguments arguments) { /* ... */ }

Dart_NativeFunction ResolveName(Dart_Handle name,
                                int argc,
                                bool* auto_setup_scope) {
    if (!Dart_IsString(name)) return NULL;

    Dart_NativeFunction result = NULL;
    if (auto_setup_scope == NULL) return NULL;

    Dart_EnterScope();
    // Convert Dart's String object to C char array.
    const char* cname;
    HandleError(Dart_StringToCString(name, &cname));
    // Return reference to Hello() function from this extension.
    if (strcmp("Hello", cname) == 0) {
        result = Hello;
    }
    Dart_ExitScope();
    return result;
}
```

We also defined a `HandleError()` helper function that checks Dart's internal `Dart_Handle` structure for an error and lets us throw a Dart exception that can be properly handled with a try-catch in Dart. The `Dart_Handle` structure represents all values in Dart. Every time we pass values from Dart or return values to Dart, we need to wrap them as `Dart_Handle` structures (for example, we had to unwrap Dart's `String` to `char*` with `Dart_StringToCString()`).

The Dart code loads the extension and maps the `_hello()` function to `Hello()` in the extension:

```
// Use dart-ext to load the native extension.
// Native extension must be libfuzzy_search.[dll, so, dylib].
import 'dart-ext:fuzzy_search';
String _hello(String str) native "Hello";

main() {
  print(_hello());
}
```

The `native` keyword makes the Dart VM call `ResolveName()`, which returns a reference to the `Hello()` function. The last thing is to implement `Hello()`:

```
char* reverse(const char* s) {
    int length = strlen(s);
    char* reverse = (char*)malloc(sizeof(char) * (length + 1));
    for (int i = 0; i < length; i++) {
        reverse[i] = s[length - 1 - i];
    }
    reverse[length] = '\0';
    return reverse;
}

void Hello(Dart_NativeArguments arguments) {
    Dart_EnterScope();
    const char* inputStr;
    char* reverseStr;
    Dart_StringToCString(
        Dart_GetNativeArgument(arguments, 0), &inputStr);
    reverseStr = reverse(inputStr);
```

```
Dart_Handle result = Dart_NewStringFromCString(reverseStr);
free(reverseStr);
Dart_SetReturnValue(arguments, result);
Dart_ExitScope();
}
```

We used the `Dart_StringToCString()` function to convert Dart's representation of `String` into an array of chars, which is stored in the `inputStr` variable. Then, we create a new array and copy all chars to it in reverse order. To return the value to Dart, we need to convert it into `Dart_Handle` with `Dart_NewStringFromCString()` and then call `Dart_SetReturnValue()`, which sets the returned value. Note that even if we didn't want to return any value, we would still have to set the return value as `null` with `Dart_SetReturnValue(Dart_Null())`.

At the beginning of the `Hello()` function, we create a new Dart scope with `Dart_EnterScope()`, which we close at the end with `Dart_ExitScope()`. This automatically deallocates all created `Dart_Handles` and we don't need to do it by ourselves as with `reverseStr`, where we have to release the allocated memory with `free(reverseStr)`.

Writing a native fuzzy search implementation

This is where things start to get interesting. When working with existing C++ code, you'll probably want to work with multiple instances of the same class, but we can't just instantiate a C++ class in Dart. Instead, we'll crate a wrapper class in Dart that stores the memory address of the C++ object. Let's start by creating a C++ class with a native fuzzy search implementation:

```cpp
// fuzzy_search.hpp
class FuzzySearch {
public:
    FuzzySearch(Dart_Handle inputItems);
    std::vector<char*> search(const char* term);
    size_t size();
private:
    char** items;
    size_t length
};
```

This is our header file. Header files in C/C++ are commonly used to define interfaces of libraries. In practice, we can use functions and data structures without worrying about their implementation. Previously, we used `dart_api.h`, which defines, for example, `Dart_Handle` or `Dart_SetReturnValue()`:

```cpp
// fuzzy_search.cpp
#include <vector>
#include "fuzzy_search.hpp"
#include "include/dart_api.h"

FuzzySearch::FuzzySearch(Dart_Handle inputList) {
    intptr_t length_ptr;

    Dart_ListLength(inputList, &length_ptr);
    length = length_ptr;
    // Allocate memory for an array of C strings.
    items = (char**)malloc(length * sizeof(char*));

    for (int i = 0; i < length; i++) {
        const char* cname;
        // Convert Dart's String to char*.
        Dart_StringToCString(
            Dart_ListGetAt(inputList, i), &cname);
        // Allocate memory for the string + termination flag.
        items[i] = (char*)malloc(strlen(cname) + 1);
        strcpy(items[i], cname);
    }
}

bool fuzzy_search(const char* item, const char* term) {
    // Same approach as fuzzy search in Chapter 2.
    size_t term_lng = strlen(term);
    size_t item_lng = strlen(item);
    int ti = 0; // term index
    // int si = 0; // key index
    for (int si = 0; si < item_lng; si++) {
        if (term[ti] == item[si] && ++ti == term_lng) {
            return true;
        }
    }
    return false;
}
```

```
std::vector<char*> FuzzySearch::search(const char* term) const {
    std::vector<char*> results;
    for (int i = 0; i < size(); i++) {
        if (fuzzy_search(items[i], term)) {
            results.push_back(items[i]);
        }
    }
    return results;
}

size_t FuzzySearch::size() {
    return length;
}
```

The search algorithm is the same as the one we used in *Chapter 2, Practical Dart*. The
`FuzzySearch::search()` method returns a `std::vector<char*>` object, which is
a resizable list that we'll later convert to a Dart `List` object. In the constructor, we
allocated an array of pointers to arrays of characters (a 2D array) representing each
searchable item.

Then, we create two functions accessible from Dart. The first one will create a new
instance of `FuzzySearch`, and the second one will perform a single search:

```
// main.cpp
void FuzzySearchCreate(Dart_NativeArguments arguments) {
    Dart_EnterScope();
    Dart_Handle inputList = Dart_GetNativeArgument(arguments, 0);

    FuzzySearch *fuzzy = new FuzzySearch(inputList);
    // Return pointer to the object (memory address).
    Dart_Handle result = Dart_NewInteger((int64_t)fuzzy);
    Dart_SetReturnValue(arguments, result);
    Dart_ExitScope();
}

void FuzzySearchSearch(Dart_NativeArguments args) {
    Dart_EnterScope();
    int64_t ptr;
    const char* term;
    Dart_IntegerToInt64(Dart_GetNativeArgument(args, 0), &ptr);
    Dart_StringToCString(Dart_GetNativeArgument(args, 1), &term);

    // Get the instance of FuzzySearch at this memory address.
    FuzzySearch *fuzzy = reinterpret_cast<FuzzySearch*>ptr;
    std::vector<char*> results = fuzzy->search(term);
```

```
        Dart_Handle result = Dart_NewList(results.size());
        for (int i = 0; i < results.size(); i++) {
            Dart_ListSetAt(result, i,
                Dart_NewStringFromCString(results.at(i)));
        }
        Dart_SetReturnValue(args, result);
        Dart_ExitScope();
    }
```

Note what we're actually returning from `FuzzySearchCreate()`. It's not an object but just an integer with a memory address of a `FuzzySearch` instance in the memory. Then, in `FuzzySearchSearch()`, we pass this address as an argument and use type casting to get the proper instance of `FuzzySearch`. Running `search()` returns a vector of `char*`, so we need to create an empty list first and fill it with Dart strings. Also, we need to know the exact size of a Dart list before creating it.

The Dart code is just a wrapper class:

```
// lib/fuzzy_search/fuzzy_search.dart
import 'dart-ext:fuzzy_search';

// All access to native functions is done via NativeFuzzySearch
// class and never directly.
int _create(List terms) native "FuzzySearchCreate";
List<String> _search(int ptr, term) native "FuzzySearchSearch";

class NativeFuzzySearch implements FuzzySearchInterface {
  int _pointer;

  NativeFuzzySearch(List terms) {
    _pointer = _create(terms);
  }

  List<String> search(String term) => _search(_pointer, term);
}
```

 The `int` built-in type is a 32-bit or 64-bit integer depending on the Dart VM build. As our native extension has to be built for the same architecture, the pointer always fits into its range.

We can use this wrapper class just like any other class in Dart without even noticing that under the hood, there are some pointers passing here and there:

```
import 'package:Chapter_09/fuzzy_search/fuzzy_search.dart';

main() {
  List<String> dict = ['item1', 'item2', ...];
  NativeFuzzySearch nativeFuzzy = new NativeFuzzySearch(dict);
  List<String> results = nativeFuzzy.search('test_term');
  print(results);
}
```

In order to test and compare the performance of both Dart and C/C++ implementations, we'll use the same dataset from *Chapter 2, Practical Dart*, but we'll replicate it more than 20 times, run a couple of test searches over it multiple times, and print average processing time for each of them (the complete benchmarking code is among the source code for this chapter):

```
Testing FuzzySearch (199034 items):
average: 18 ms

Testing NativeFuzzySearch (199034 items):
average: 13 ms
```

We can see that the native implementation is about 28 percent faster.

 We're measuring the processing time by ourselves, which is easier for demonstration purposes. If you're looking for a more standardized environment, take a look at https://github.com/dart-lang/benchmark_harness.

Optimizing our C/C++ code

However, there are some optimization tricks that we can use.

We allocate memory for every single item in the list with malloc(). This is correct, but the bottleneck is that items are shattered all over the memory. Each access to memory retrieves not just the exact amount of bytes that we need but an entire memory word (typically, 4 bytes on 32-bit systems and 8 bytes on 64-bit systems). Loaded memory words are saved into the processor's L1-3 caches.

This implies that when we have, for example, a 9-character long string, it requires 2 memory accesses on a 64-bit system where the second memory access is required to load just one byte. Therefore, when we're iterating the entire array of char*, it's better to allocate one large memory block for all the items. A better version of our constructor will look like:

```cpp
FuzzySearch::FuzzySearch(Dart_Handle inputList) {
    intptr_t length_ptr;
    // Get Dart's List length.
    Dart_ListLength(inputList, &length_ptr);
    length = length_ptr;

    items = (char**)malloc(length * sizeof(char*));

    // Calculate total size of all items in bytes.
    uint32_t size = 0;
    for (int i = 0; i < length; i++) {
        const char* cname;
        Dart_StringToCString(
            Dart_ListGetAt(inputList, i), &cname);
        size += strlen(cname) + 1;
    }
    // Allocate one large block of memory.
    char* ptr = (char*)malloc(size * sizeof(char));

    for (int i = 0; i < length; i++) {
        const char* cname;
        Dart_StringToCString(
            Dart_ListGetAt(inputList, i), &cname);
        items[i] = ptr;
        strcpy(items[i], cname);
        // Increment the pointer.
        ptr += strlen(cname) + 1;
    }
}
```

With this updated version, the average search time is about 11.5 ms.

 In order to keep the examples simple, we're not checking returned values from `malloc()` or `Dart_StringToCString()`, which in a real application should be checked for error code.

But we can go even further. We can make use of multiple cores without any manual splitting and merging C++ vectors for each core by ourselves. We'll make use of the OpenMP 4.0 standard that is supported, for example, in GNU GCC 4.9 compiler and modify the `search()` method with two new statements for the precompiler:

```
std::vector<char*> FuzzySearch::search(const char* term) {
    #pragma omp declare reduction (merge : std::vector<char*> : \
      omp_out.insert(omp_out.end(), omp_in.begin(), omp_in.end()))
    std::vector<char*> results;

    #pragma omp parallel for reduction(merge: results)
    for (int i = 0; i < length; i++) {
        if (fuzzy_search(items[i], term)) {
            results.push_back(items[i]);
        }
    }
    return results;
}
```

These two `#pragma omp` statements are ignored by compilers that don't support OpenMP. As `vector<T>` is not thread-safe, we create a private instance for each thread and then merge all of them into one `vector<T>` result. OpenMP does all this automatically without modifying our code at all. We could hardcode how many threads will be spawned, but OpenMP can read the `OMP_NUM_THREADS` environment variable for how many threads to spawn in each parallel block so that we can easily test what's the best number for us.

On Intel Code Duo 2.5 GHz, the best results occur with four threads that give 5.1 ms on average. At the end, our native implementation is 3.5 times faster than the Dart code running in the Dart VM. Note that the standalone Dart VM has much better performance than Dartium.

We could also use compiler options such as **strict aliasing** to optimize the usage of pointers or try to work with ifs and loops for better **branch prediction**, but this level of optimization is generally considered for developers with no friends.

Multithreading with Dart Isolates

Although Dart doesn't have C-style threads, we can still make use of multiple CPUs and cores with Dart Isolates using the built-in `dart:isolate` library that works both in the browser (using Web Workers) and in the standalone Dart VM. Every Dart app has at least one Isolate called root.

Unlike threads, Isolates don't share the same memory space, so they can't modify each other's variables and all communication between them must be done via message passing.

We're not going to go into it here because it wouldn't help us very much. There are no C-style thread locks for Isolates, so synchronizing multiple Isolates would be rather difficult. There's not much documentation available for Isolates right now, so the only way to get to know anything about it is in the Dart API at `https://api.dartlang.org/apidocs/channels/stable/dartdoc-viewer/dart:isolate.Isolate`.

There's also an experimental Dart runtime in development called **Fletch** that promises very high concurrency (`https://github.com/dart-lang/fletch`).

Writing bindings for the exiv2 library

There are thousands of libraries already written in C/C++ and used in practice, sometimes for decades. Therefore, it doesn't make sense to try to write everything from scratch. Of course, if you want to run your code in the browser, you have to rewrite it into Dart, but in cases where you're only interested in server-side scripting, you can reuse existing C/C++ code, wrap it with a small native extension, and use it in Dart.

In this example, we'll use `exiv2`, which is a library written in C++ that can read and modify the EXIF metadata from pictures. This is, for example, what camera vendor and model you used, the exposure time, and so on:

```cpp
// main.cpp
// Header file is a part of exiv2 source code.
#include "exiv2.hpp"

void GetExifRecord(Dart_NativeArguments arguments) {
    Dart_EnterScope();

    const char *filename;
    const char *tag;
    Dart_StringToCString(
        Dart_GetNativeArgument(arguments, 0), &filename);
    Dart_StringToCString(
        Dart_GetNativeArgument(arguments, 1), &tag);

    Exiv2::Image::AutoPtr image =
        Exiv2::ImageFactory::open(filename);
    image->readMetadata();
```

```cpp
    Exiv2::ExifData &exifData = image->exifData();
    Exiv2::ExifKey key = Exiv2::ExifKey(tag);
    Exiv2::ExifData::const_iterator pos = exifData.findKey(key);

    Dart_Handle result;

    if (pos == exifData.end()) { // not found
        result = Dart_Null();
    } else {
        result = Dart_NewStringFromCString(
            pos->value().toString().c_str());
    }

    Dart_SetReturnValue(arguments, result);
    Dart_ExitScope();
}


void GetAllExifRecords(Dart_NativeArguments args) {
    Dart_EnterScope();

    const char *fname;
    Dart_StringToCString(Dart_GetNativeArgument(args, 0), &fname);

    Exiv2::Image::AutoPtr image =
        Exiv2::ImageFactory::open(fname);
    image->readMetadata();
    Exiv2::ExifData &exifData = image->exifData();
    Exiv2::ExifData::const_iterator end = exifData.end();
    Exiv2::ExifData::const_iterator pointer = exifData.begin();

    Dart_Handle result = Dart_NewList(exifData.count());
    // Iterate all EXIF records.
    for (int j = 0; pointer != end; ++pointer, j++) {
        // Create \t delimetered char*.
        std::stringstream fmt;
        fmt << pointer->key() << "\t" << pointer->value();
        const char *record = fmt.str().c_str();
        Dart_ListSetAt(result, j,
            Dart_NewStringFromCString(record));
    }

    Dart_SetReturnValue(args, result);
    Dart_ExitScope();
}
```

We created two functions. The first one returns a specific EXIF record by its tag name. The second one creates a list of all tags and records delimited by the \t character. Right now, there's no easy way to create a Dart's Map object and set its key-value pairs in a native extension, so we'll process the List object later in Dart.

The rest of the C++ code is the same as in the previous examples. The Dart code just wraps all calls to the extension:

```
// lib/exiv2/exiv2.dart
import 'dart-ext:exiv2_wrapper';

List<String> _all(String filename) native "GetAllExifRecords";
String _get(String filename, String tag) native "GetExifRecord";

Map<String, String> all(String filename) {
  Map<String, String> map = {};
  _all(filename).forEach((String record) {
    List kv = record.split('\t');
    map[kv[0]] = kv[1];
  });
  return map;
}


String get(String filename, String tag) {
  return _get(filename, tag);
}
```

We wrapped calls to _all() with a function that converts Dart's List object into a Map object. Let's test our extension with the following code:

```
import 'package:Chapter_09_exiv2/exiv2/exiv2.dart' as exiv2;
import 'dart:io';

main() {
  String path = Platform.script.resolve('img.jpg').toFilePath();
  exiv2.all(path).forEach((String key, String value) {
    print("$key = $value");
  });
  print(exiv2.get(path, 'Exif.Photo.ExposureTime'));
}
```

The result looks something like this:

```
$ dart main.dart
Exif.Image.Make = Canon
Exif.Image.Model = Canon EOS 550D
Exif.Image.Orientation = 1
...
Exif.Photo.WhiteBalance = 1
Exif.Photo.SceneCaptureType = 0
1/250
```

As of now (May 2015), the Dart package repository doesn't contain any EXIF manipulation library written in Dart.

Distributing native extensions

The obvious questions are how can we give our extensions to someone or how can we use somebody's native extension? Currently, there's no unified way for this, and we have to download extensions and compile them by ourselves. This also includes all third-party libraries that the extension is using and can't be distributed with the extension because these have to be built specifically for our platform and architecture.

There's a `https://pub.dartlang.org/packages/ccompile` project that looks promising and may become a universal build tool for Dart's native extensions in the future.

Summary

Writing native extensions for the standalone Dart VM isn't that hard. It requires some previous knowledge of C/C++ and ideally compilers as well, but the approach is very straightforward and the potential is limited only by your imagination.

Native extensions for Dart are quite specific and you're definitely not going to use them every day, but it's good to know that you can reuse a lot of existing libraries written in C/C++ and achieve very good performance when you need it.

Index

Symbols

E

exceptions
about 20
static types, using 20
exiv2 library
bindings, writing for 198-201

F

Factory design pattern 98
formatters
about 128
filter 128
orderBy 128
functions 17

G

generative constructors 19
GeoLocation API
using 81
Google Cloud Platform 2
Google Maps API
using 81

H

handleMessage()method 147
handleWebSocket() method 147
HTML5 DeviceOrientation events
3D bookshelf, creating with 74-80
HTML Import
about 91
implementing 91-94
HTTP server
writing, with route package 158-161

I

idb.KeyRange item 57
IndexedDB
about 52
application, polishing 58
indices 56, 57
initializing 53, 54

records, deleting 56
records, saving 55
restrictions 52, 53
stored records, fetching 54, 55
Isolate API 68

J

JSONP data, Reddit Read Later app
fetching 48-51

K

Kalman filter 85
Karma
about 181
URL 181

L

life cycle methods, polymer.dart
attached() 106
attributeChanged() 106
CustomElement.created() 106
detached() 106
ready() 106
LocalStorage
versus IndexedDB 58

M

matchers
completes 168
contains 168
equals 168
equalsIgnoringCase 168
hasLength 168
isEmpty 168
isIn 168
isInstanceOf<T> 168
orderedEquals 168
reference link 169
returnsNormally 168
same 168
throws 168
unorderedEquals 168

mixins
about 179, 180
URL 179
Model-View-Controller (MVC) 115
music visualizer app
about 47, 59
creating 59-64
MVW (Model-View-Whatever)
about 116
URL 116

N

named constructors 19
named parameters
defining 17
native extensions, for standalone Dart VM
<extension_name>_Init() function 187
asynchronous extension 188
distributing 201
minimal native extension, writing 188-191
ResolveName() function 188
structure 187, 188
synchronous extension 188
URL 188
writing 187
native fuzzy search implementation
C/C++ code, optimizing 195-197
Dart Isolates, multithreading with 197
writing 191-195
ng-repeat directive 128

O

Observatory tool
profiling with 182-185
one-way data binding
{{coverImage}} 105
{{rotateYString}} 105
about 104-108
loops and conditions, in templates 108, 109
on-click 105
onTouch events
used, for drawing into 2D canvas 86, 87
operator overloading
about 178, 179
reference link 179

P

parameters 17
performance tips, AngularDart
about 136, 137
DOM tree modification, avoiding 138, 139
excess formatter usage, avoiding 138
nesting ng-repeat directives, avoiding 137
track by, using for ng-repeat 138
Photon
about 80
URL 80
play_phaser library
about 68
URL 68
polymer.dart
about 101
life cycle methods 106
minimalistic custom element 101-103
Polymer
core-list 111-113
core and paper elements 111
URL, for tutorials 114
position and distance tracker
with GeoLocation API and
    Google Maps API 81-85
process ID (PID) 152
properties, ng-repeat directive
$even 133
$first 133
$index 133
$last 133
$middle 133
$odd 133
Protractor 181
pubspec.yaml files
URL 33

R

Reddit API
about 49
URL 49
Reddit Read Later app
about 47
creating 48

Thank you for buying
Dart Essentials

About Packt Publishing

Packt, pronounced 'packed', published its first book, *Mastering phpMyAdmin for Effective MySQL Management*, in April 2004, and subsequently continued to specialize in publishing highly focused books on specific technologies and solutions.

Our books and publications share the experiences of your fellow IT professionals in adapting and customizing today's systems, applications, and frameworks. Our solution-based books give you the knowledge and power to customize the software and technologies you're using to get the job done. Packt books are more specific and less general than the IT books you have seen in the past. Our unique business model allows us to bring you more focused information, giving you more of what you need to know, and less of what you don't.

Packt is a modern yet unique publishing company that focuses on producing quality, cutting-edge books for communities of developers, administrators, and newbies alike. For more information, please visit our website at www.packtpub.com.

About Packt Open Source

In 2010, Packt launched two new brands, Packt Open Source and Packt Enterprise, in order to continue its focus on specialization. This book is part of the Packt Open Source brand, home to books published on software built around open source licenses, and offering information to anybody from advanced developers to budding web designers. The Open Source brand also runs Packt's Open Source Royalty Scheme, by which Packt gives a royalty to each open source project about whose software a book is sold.

Writing for Packt

We welcome all inquiries from people who are interested in authoring. Book proposals should be sent to author@packtpub.com. If your book idea is still at an early stage and you would like to discuss it first before writing a formal book proposal, then please contact us; one of our commissioning editors will get in touch with you.

We're not just looking for published authors; if you have strong technical skills but no writing experience, our experienced editors can help you develop a writing career, or simply get some additional reward for your expertise.

Learning Dart

ISBN: 978-1-84969-742-2   Paperback: 388 pages

Learn how to program applications with Dart 1.0, a language specifically designed to produce better-structured, high-performance applications

1. Develop apps for the Web using Dart and HTML5.

2. Build powerful HTML5 forms, validate and store data in local storage, and use web components to build your own user interface.

3. Make games by drawing and integrate audio and video in the browser.

4. Learn how to develop an application with the help of a model-driven and fast-paced approach.

Mastering Dart

ISBN: 978-1-78398-956-0   Paperback: 346 pages

Master the art of programming high-performance applications with Dart

1. Improve the performance of your Dart code and build sophisticated applications.

2. Enhance your web projects by adding advanced HTML 5 features.

3. Full of solutions to real-world problems, with clear explanations for complicated concepts of Dart.

Please check **www.PacktPub.com** for information on our titles

Dart Cookbook

ISBN: 978-1-78398-962-1   Paperback: 346 pages

Over 110 incredibly effective, useful, and hands-on recipes to design Dart web client and server applications

1. Develop stunning apps for the modern web using Dart.

2. Learn how to store your app's data in common SQL and NoSQL databases with Dart.

3. Create state-of-the-art web apps with Polymer and Angular.

RESTful Java Web Services

ISBN: 978-1-84719-646-0   Paperback: 256 pages

Master core REST concepts and create RESTful web services in Java

1. Build powerful and flexible RESTful web services in Java using the most popular Java RESTful frameworks to date (Restlet, JAX-RS based frameworks Jersey and RESTEasy, and Struts 2).

2. Master the concepts to help you design and implement RESTful web services.

3. Plenty of screenshots and clear explanations to facilitate learning.

Please check **www.PacktPub.com** for information on our titles

www.ingramcontent.com/pod-product-compliance
Lightning Source LLC
Chambersburg PA
CBHW060549060326
40690CB00017B/3657